Writers
on
Islands

An anthology edited by
James Knox Whittet

IRON PRESS

First published 2008 by IRON Press

5 Marden Terrace, Cullercoats
Northumberland, NE30 4PD
tel/fax: +44 (0)191 253 1901
ironpress@blueyonder.co.uk
www.ironpress.co.uk

ISBN 978-0-9552450-5-3
Printed by rpm print & design

Typeset in Garamond
Cover photograph by Armin Grewe, www.armin-grewe.com
Cover design by Brian Grogan
Book layout by Kate Jones

IRON Press books are distributed by Central Books
and represented by Inpress Limited,
Northumberland House,
11 The Pavement, Pope's Lane,
Ealing, London W5 4NG
Tel: +44 (0)20 8832 7464
Fax: +44 (0)20 8832 7465
www.inpressbooks.co.uk

To Ann

Map Index

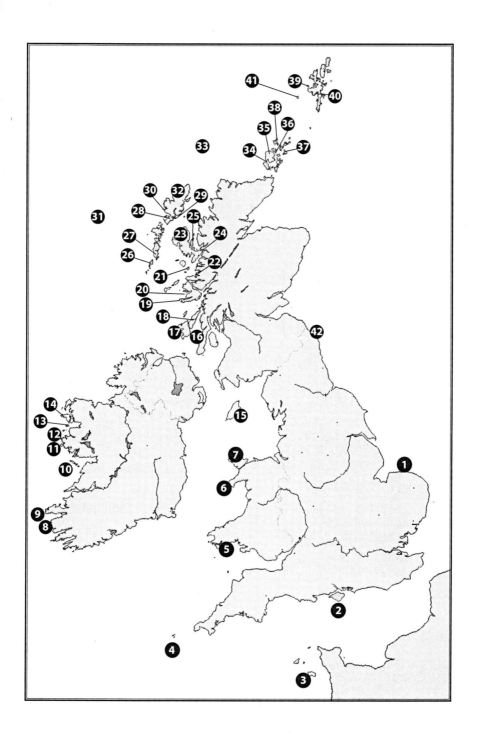

CONTENTS

FOREWORD

In a wonderful essay on his friend, John Millington Synge who lived for years on the Aran Islands which lie off the west coast of Ireland, W.B. Yeats wrote of the profound influence which this island experience had on Synge as both a man and as a writer:

Here were men and women who under the weight of necessity lived, as the artist lives, in the presence of death and childhood, and the great affections and the orgiastic moment when life outleaps its limits, and who, as it is always with those who have refused or escaped the trivial and the temporary, had dignity and good manners where manners mattered.

The aim of this anthology is to bring together the deepest emotions and reflections of those who have *refused or escaped the trivial and the temporary:* it would be difficult to think of an age when such an undertaking was more necessary.

Those words of Yeats remind us that island life is not an escape from reality but it can be a means of entering more deeply into life and death. In the sublime chapter of his autobiography in which he recaptures his childhood on the tiny, Orcadian island of Wyre, Edwin Muir writes precisely of this impossibility of escape:

In an island everything is near, for compressed within it are all the things which are spread out over a nation or continent, and there is no way of getting away from them.

A small island is a microcosm of the world and, because it is a microcosm, every aspect of life and death can be perceived with a greater clarity and intensity. The universal themes which are explored in Muir's poetry grew out of a square mile of land. To live in a small island community, you must adapt to the comforting yet terrible proximity of other people. Muir goes on to relate the deep effect which the death of a near neighbour had on his childish mind – in an island the size of Wyre, all one's neighbours are near.

A neighbouring farmer who had often brought me sweets in his snuff-lined pockets had died in great pain a little time before, and I had heard all about his death: I can still feel the terror of it.

The Catholic priest, Angus John MacQueen who grew up in South Uist, in the Outer Hebrides, also talks of his childhood experiences of confronting every aspect of life and death head-on. He also talks, like Yeats, of the innate dignity of islanders who had largely escaped the more dehumanizing effects of the industrial revolution.

The great Celtic thing is that you mustn't lose your dignity. You must remember that you have great dignity as a created being and never lose that dignity. And that's why our blessing was never to have experienced the industrial revolution or the post-industrial revolution period in the Hebrides. We never lost that dignity.

In an attempt to capture the fullest possible range of island experiences, I have included in this anthology passages of the most memorable non-fiction writing by many of the most distinguished writers of the 20th and 21st centuries, alongside a number of unjustly neglected writers. I have included passages from autobiographies and biographies, letters, journals, essays, articles, travel books and accounts by naturalists. I have included revealing passages by those born and bred on islands, those who have lived for years on islands or poets such as Louis MacNiece, John Betjeman and Kathleen Jamie who have visited islands. I have included prose inspired by islands and groups of islands all around the coast of Britain and Ireland. The readers of this book will undertake a literary journey, traveling clockwise, from the small Norfolk island of Scolt Head to the Isle of Wight, the Channel Isles, the Scilly Isles, Lundy, the Pembrokeshire islands and Anglesey. Then we move west over to Ireland: to Skellig Michael, the Great Blaskets, the Clew Bay Islands, High Island, Achill Island and the Aran Islands. The journey takes us north to the Isle of Man, then the Inner Hebrides, the Outer Hebrides, including of course St. Kilda. We go further north to the Orkney Isles, the Shetland Isles and then make our way down the coast, ending at Lindisfarne and St. Cuthbert's Island.

I hope that those who undertake this journey will be left, like me, with unforgettable memories, including the following:

Tom Davies arrives at a Benedictine monastery on the Isle of Wight one wet evening and enters a world of silence, interspersed with bells, where men in black robes bow their cowled heads in a chapel lit by a single candle and chant Gregorian hymns. The next morning, the Abbot, after years of prayer and reflection, talks of the utter futility of trying to hold on to a fixed image of God:

Yet the closer you come, the further away God seems to be. He is nothing like his created reality. The more you understand the more you realize you don't understand. He is only like himself.

R.S. Thomas writes of his lonely, intense childhood in Anglesey and how he would make an effigy and place it on a chair at the head of the stairs to comfort him on those dark evenings when his parents had left him on his own. As Thomas rightly states: *A man's personality is a strange thing. It reveals itself in mysterious ways.*

In his cottage on Achill Island, the eminent German novelist, Heinrich Böll meditates on the dominant element of almost all our west coast islands: rain. *The rain here is absolute, magnificent, and frightening.* He wisely advises on the importance of having whisky, candles and a Bible which he consults in order to reassure himself that *the promise to send no more floods has been given.*

In a more remote cottage in Jura, George Orwell, dying of tuberculosis, creates the malevolent, all-seeing Big Brother beneath the Paps of Jura whose smoothed summits were for centuries worshipped by early islanders as the attributes of a maternal deity who benignly watched over their every move: 'Paps' is an old word for breasts. It seems appropriate that those symbols of the vigilant goddess of islanders – as viewed from the superior vantage point of Islay – should adorn the cover of this book.

The tiny Hebridean island of Inchkenneth, which lies off the west coast of Mull, was once owned by the extraordinary Mitford family and it was here that Unity Mitford – a cousin of Winston Churchill – was brought to live out her remaining years after she shot herself in the head in a park in Munich at news of the declaration of war between Britain and Germany. She had developed a passion, largely unrequited, for Adolph Hitler and, although the bullet lodged in her brain inevitably affected her memory, in her more lucid moments, she would vividly recall Adolph's beautiful blue eyes and his great liking for chocolate éclairs. Unity would sit for hour after hour on the island's pier gazing longingly out to sea.

On Eilean Shona, a small island south of Skye where J.M. Barrie lived from time to time in the island's mansion, we find the outstanding naturalist, Mike Tomkies living alone in the island's shack, having turned his back on his former glamorous life as a successful Hollywood journalist. After a solitary Christmas lunch, he recalls the answer given by Brigitte Bardot when he had asked her if, despite her considerable fame and numerous romances, she ever felt lonely:

Everybody is really alone. You are always alone. You are alone when you are born and you are alone when you die. All your life you are alone. To me it is normal.

On the high island of Hoy, we find Peter Maxwell Davies, perhaps Britain's finest living composer who was drawn to make a home in the Orkney Isles by the writings of George MacKay Brown, living in a cottage on a cliff and hearing daily the thunder of the sea and the lonely cries of sea birds: sounds which have come to permeate much of his music.

Still further north, on the bleak Shetland island of Whalsay we encounter the great Scots poet, Hugh MacDiarmid who lived there in considerable poverty for most of the 1930s He had arrived on the island in a still more penniless condition: *I could not have lived anywhere else that is known to me these last four years without recourse to the poorhouse.* Although he came to the island physically and psychologically a broken man, gradually, through contact with the crofters and fishermen of the island, he found a kind of healing and wrote some of his finest poems on Whalsay.

The above are just a few of the many memorable encounters in this journey around our coast. This is of course a deeply personal anthology in that I have chosen only those passages which appeal to me in the hope that at least some of them will appeal to others. If an anthology is not truly personal, it's not anything.

If living on an island or going to live on an island is an escape from anything, it is an escape from homogeneity and categorization. An island anthology should be a celebration of difference. Through travel and reading, I have been struck by the astonishing variety of our islands in terms of people, culture and landscape. Such an awareness makes one cautious about making too many generalizations about islands and the people who live on them. It is as if the barrier of the sea allows people to retain more of their sense of individuality. Sheila Gear who has lived most of her life in one of the most individual island communities of them all: Foula, expresses this sense of a small island's freedom from conformity – and the economic price paid for such freedom:

Modern industrial society, if it is to be efficient economically, requires its people to conform to a uniform standard. It's bureaucracy has no use for the small group whose needs are different, who cannot be tidily lumped in with the others.

There is also a sense in which many islanders escape from the insidious demands of nationalism which has been such a murderous force in the 20th century and continues to be so in the 21st century. The boundaries of fervent nationalists are often somewhat vague, as vague as their ambitions, whereas on a small island the boundaries are clearly defined, you live within sight of them. Indeed, it is this sense of geographical completeness which is the essence of island living. Attending a small primary school in the Hebridean island of Islay, I was confronted each day with a large map of Islay – not of Scotland or of Britain – on the wall in front of me. The shape of the island, its villages, its hills, its principal sea lochs and hill lochs were studied in detail. My teacher who was an amateur archaeologist recounted the lives and dwellings of early islanders. The country of which Islay was a part of was not my country: it was an alien, if sometimes enticing land. The poet, Iain Crichton Smith who grew up in the Isle of Lewis in the 1930s and 40s also writes of his sense of national alienation:

I had no feeling for Scotland at all as a country except through football. I did not feel myself as belonging to Scotland. I felt myself as belonging to Lewis. I had never even seen a train. I had never been out of the island in my whole life. Glasgow was as distant to me as the moon.

London, with its warmongering politicians, would of course have seemed far more distant still.

The first piece of prose in this anthology, before our journey begins, is by Gavin Maxwell. In the first chapter of his autobiography, *Harpoon At A Venture*, he recalls a particular day when he was stationed in London in 1940, during the Battle of Britain, and in the midst of an interminable bombing raid with death and destruction all around him. Having himself narrowly escaped death, he suddenly makes a resolution:

If I'm alive when the war's over I'm going to buy an island in the Hebrides and retire there for life; no aeroplanes, no bombs, no Commanding Officer, no rusty dannert wire.

He unfolds a map of Scotland on the floor and recites the lyrical and evocative names of Hebridean islands aloud: Hyskeir, Rona, Canna, Staffa, like a devout Catholic telling his beads. He draws a red ring around each island and then draws a second ring around Soay: the first of the islands he was to live on, as soon as the war ended. Further on in this book, we meet with Maxwell again towards the end of his life, living on the still smaller Hebridean island of Eilean Bhan – The White Island.

Of course, as books such as Tom Freeman-Keel's *From Auschwitz To Alderney* forcibly remind us, a British island can itself be turned into death camp. Nonetheless, the lure of life on a remote island will always be inextricably bound up with a desire to escape from the insanity of the rest of the world.

The longing to set foot on a small island, particularly a remote and abandoned one with its deserted cemetery seems to me to be closely related to the need which many feel, whether or not they are believers, to visit churches with their surrounding dead. As Charles MacLean reminds us in his moving description of the graveyard on St. Kilda: *Deserted cemeteries often enjoy a longer half-life than the ruins of places where people have lived.* There is deep within all of us an unquenchable desire *to be more serious*, to borrow Philip Larkin's words in *Church Going*, and, to repeat those opening words of Yeats, *to escape the trivial.*

With her usual insight, Kathleen Raine perceived that the philosophical materialism which had come to dominate 'mainland' thought had debased the arts themselves. When she first visits the Hebridean Isle of Eigg in the 1950s, she is compelled by the nature of the island's atmosphere, light, landscape and culture where *Homer might have sung in those kitchens by turf fires* to ask:

Is there a spiritual geography, are there certain places upon the earth which are more or less attuned to certain modes of consciousness?

I believe that many of the islands around our coast are attuned to different *modes of consciousness* and that this is the primary justification for an anthology devoted to islands which are too often neglected by city-centered opinion makers. It is not only writers, artists and musicians who have felt this but the many monks, mystics and other contemplatives who sought on islands throughout the centuries that *desert of the ocean on thin places* where the material and the spiritual seems to merge.

I have ended this anthology with a short chapter by John MacLeod entitled *But Still We Sing*. Although MacLeod speaks in particular of the continuing defiance of Hebridean islanders in the face of centuries of injustice, suppression and economic neglect by a succession of ignorant and patronizing mainlanders, it can speak for many of the islanders who live, more or less precariously, on pieces of land all around the coast of Britain and Ireland. All the varied voices contained in this book might be heard as contributing to a cycle of distinctive island songs. Describing the most hauntingly beautiful of all our island songs: the Gaelic psalms, most closely associated with the Free Presbyterian Church whose spiritual heartland is on the islands of Lewis and Harris, the Australian writer, Rosemary Millington writes:

I heard the music on this Sunday that I had never heard before, except in my dream. As exuberantly as bugles the voices came from every heart, some stridently unblending with voices accustomed to singing above the wind on the moor and ocean.

According to Euripides, humans suffer so that the goddesses might compose beautiful songs but it's not only the goddesses who sing out of suffering – as well as out of a sense of defiance, freedom and joy. I hope that those readers who, for whatever reason, will never set foot on any of the remoter islands encountered in this book will at least catch something of the harmony and counterpoint of our enduring island songs.

James Knox Whittet, 2008

Islands

Gavin Maxwell, best known as the author of 'A Ring Of Bright Water', describes a profound turning point in his life after a close brush with death. Like many people, he dreams of buying a small island and living out of reach of bombs and barbed wire.

The Scent of Turf Smoke

Gavin Maxwell

This story begins in 1940. We were stationed in the South Metropolitan Gas Works on the riverside just below Blackwall Tunnel and opposite the East India Dock; a detachment of three officers and two hundred men as a nominally mobile anti-parachute column.

It was the third week of the Battle of Britain blitz, and we were tired and nostalgic. I had been doing a round of our extensive perimeter. The raid had been continuous throughout the night; at about three a.m. a single note had suddenly become separated from the welter of sound – a falling bomb almost directly overhead. It caused my Commanding Officer to say briefly, "This is our lot at last," as we dived for the nearest cover. The noise increased to a sort of gobbling roar, then the ground shook and shuddered, but there was no explosion.

"Another U.X.B.," he said disgustedly, "and a monster, by the sound of it. Someone'll have to go and look for that one as soon as it's light."

I went out an hour later in the uncanny quiet of the All Clear. The dawns were always the same in that brilliant September – cloudless, calm, with the silver barrage-balloons floating on a pale, radiant sky. I looked for the bomb-hole for a long time without success. Everywhere was the rubble and confusion of former raids; last night a paper factory had received a direct hit, and over a wide area its contents blanketed the ground and the rubble like dirty snow. I was on my way back to report failure when I turned into the churchyard, saw the great well-shaft ten feet across among the gravestones, and remembered with a sickening lurch of the heart that the crypt was in use as a shelter. I ran down the long winding steps and struggled with the door. As it burst open under my weight I was hit by a stifling wave of air so noisome that I retched even at its first impact. The temperature was that of a Kew hothouse, the stench indescribable. As I became accustomed to the dim light I saw that the stone floor was swimming in urine, and between the packed human forms were piles of excrement and of vomit. One hundred and twelve people had been in that airless crypt for seven hours. They were not anxious to be disturbed; abusive voices, thick with sleep, told me to close the doors. I had just time to open both wide before I was myself sick, helplessly and endlessly.

When I came in I went to my bedroom, which had been one of the make-up rooms of the Gas Works private theatre and was lined with mirrors. Coated with the dust of blast, I looked much like the publican whose corpse I had seen removed the day before from the ruins of his pub on the corner. I got a towel and went down to the communal shower-baths; took off my clothes and elbowed my way between two naked Guardsmen, one of whom stood ludicrously to attention. I told him with some embarrassment that it was unnecessary, but he remained as though he had not heard me. After a moment the corporal on my other side said, "You have to speak very slowly, sir; he comes from the Hebrides, and he doesn't understand very easily." I tried again more slowly; he relaxed sheepishly and went on soaping himself. I asked him from which island he came. It was a small island in the Outer Hebrides; I did not know it, but I had seen it from the sea, and the name and his soft speech brought a momentary vision of its low hulk dark against a harsh Atlantic sunset.

When I had dressed and gone up to the tiny windowless room which served us for anteroom and mess, my thoughts were far away. One of my brother officers was there reading a yellow-back. I said, "I've made a resolution. If I'm alive when the war's over I'm going to buy an island in the Hebrides and retire there for life; no aeroplanes, no bombs, no Commanding Officer, no rusty dannert wire."

"And no leave, and no friends, and no pay. But I'll join you. Let's look at a map."

Deep in a spirit of nursery make-believe, we spread a map of Scotland on the floor, and like children lay at full length before it, propped on our elbows. We started at the north of the map and worked down. It took a long time; we found many places that we knew. I remember the atmosphere of the room vividly, and the comparison that my mind drew with the island pictures painted by my hyperactive imagination. In the mess it was stuffy and airless, for the only lighting and ventilation came from a skylight which had to be kept permanently blacked out. The room was lit by gas, whose constant hiss meant to me for a long time only Blackwall and blitz; now the louder hiss of Tilley lamps in boats and in crofts has overlaid that impression with more pleasant ones. There was an intermittent buzz of drowsy bluebottles, and the walls were spotted black with their remains. The room was tiny; my recollection is that we occupied most of it by lying at full length.

We spoke of Hyskeir, Rona, Canna, Staffa; in my mind were high-pluming seas bursting upon Atlantic cliffs and booming thunderously into tunnelled caverns; eider-ducks among the surf; gannets fishing in deep blue water; and, landward, the scent of turf smoke.

After an hour there were rings drawn round several islands. I had drawn an extra red ring round the Island of Soay, an island unknown to either of us, below the Cuillin of Skye. We were still playing at make-believe; Soay was my Island Valley of Avalon, and Avalon was all the world away. Presently the sirens sounded, and down the river the guns began again.

Scolt Head

We begin our clockwise journey around the coast of Britain and Ireland with the tiny island of Scolt Head which lies just off the coast of Norfolk, in the company of Kevin Crossley-Holland in his search for 'adventure, solitude and beauty'.

The Stability Of Islands
Kevin Crossley-Holland

The first island to make its mark on me lies in the middle of a creek in that part of England I love best, North Norfolk. It is perhaps a hundred yards long, twenty yards wide, a long grassy hummock fringed by reeds and samphire and mud. Day after day through my early childhood my sister and I used to paddle or row across to it, depending on the state of the tide; it was ours, and with great ceremony we christened it 'Kenwood' in honour of the name of the chocolate bars we had taken to eat there.

At the height of one spring tide, I was on the island fishing, exploiting my sister as a gillie. My rod thrashed the air; my line whirled like a dervish; I cast, and the hook lodged in my thumb. It was then that I appreciated for the first time the extreme importance of regular communications. What happens when the oarsmen has landed his thumb, when the gillie cannot row, when the engine breaks down, when the elements take over? This is a recurring theme in my book.

In time, I graduated to the island at the creek's mouth, Scolt Head, a magnificent complex of sand dune, shingle ridge and saltmarsh that is now maintained as a bird reserve by the National Trust.

Walking on Scolt Head, seeing another walk there, a distant figure pinning together beach, sea, and awnings of the huge East Anglian sky, I think I first felt the need for solitude; there I first recognised the power of the natural world, above all the sea; and there I first realised, too, that an environment is only beautiful because humans think it so, and that without people (whether visitors or inhabitants) that place and any place are meaningless.

Adventure, solitude, beauty, I understood these needs before I was fifteen, and see now my two sons beginning to recognise the same need. I was sixteen when the romantic appeal of islands first enslaved me. Half-way between Sweden and Finland, half-way through the night, I was dancing to an accordion on a deck so slippery with spray that every time the boat lurched the dancers slid into a tight compress, crushed and laughing, against port or starboard rails. Then out of the blue, the dark blue, loomed the darker Aland Islands, and a huddle of cold lights. The boat closed with them, slowed, docked; there were strange shouts, lumpings and gratings; then the boat sailed on, minus my dancing partner. It was a matter of moments not hours, novel and singular. And when a few hours later I woke, the whole episode seemed dreamlike, an affair of the night, a carefree place between care and care, as improbable then as it has been unforgettable ever since.

I have been cataloguing my small experience of islands, because I believe it helps to explain why I have written this book and what it is about. Adventure, solitude, beauty, romance.... It was Murano, Burano and Torcello that made me think of small island and city in direct contrast. The escape from sluggish, fetid Venice to the fresh airs and the simple graces of those islands is exhilarating. But the need regularly to escape, that has come only in the last few years. The stress of city life, the dangers of the ghastly technosphere that man has created and now rules men, these are well-worn themes, but they have inevitably influenced my thinking and my actions. Nobody has written about them more combatively or constructively than Max Nicholson:

As nature is man's ancestral home and nurse, and as landscape is his modern mirror, the achievement of a fresh recognition by mankind of the potential for the renewal and for the healing of a sick society through creative intimacy with the natural environment could bring a transformation of the kind and scale which our degenerate and self-disgusted, materialistic, power-drunk and sex-crazed civilisation needs.

The need to escape, then, has for me become escape to the intoxication and relative stability of islands, islands which are mirrors of the human spirit, the natural world's correlatives to the human condition. And 'creative intimacy with the natural environment' has, for me, meant a growing desire better to understand the nature of small Anglo-Saxon and Celtic islands and their communities, and to write about them. These are the book's mainsprings.

Isle Of Wight

On a wet evening, Tom Davies arrives at the island's Benedictine monastery and discovers a way of life in which men embark daily on the 'long process of coming close to God'.

Lost On The Old Way

Tom Davies

It was early evening and raining on the castellated, red-brick spires of Quarr Monastery on the Isle of Wight. The rain was tadpoling down the leaded windows with the wind pounding against the doors and walls. Suddenly, two soft chimes of bells hung in the weeping night. Yet, inside the monastery walls, there was a silence which swept all around; it moved through the darkened crypt, hung around the pointed arches of the cloisters and was all but deafening in the high wide church lit by just one guttering candle. Another few bells.

Doors opened around the cloisters and men in black, billowing robes slipped silently down to the refectory. It was time for the 7.30 supper and, after bowing to the figure of Christ pinioned to the walls, some 23 of them stood behind wooden chairs as one led the Grace and the others responded. They took their knives and forks out of huge, white linen napkins which they stuffed into their collars and ate a plain meal of beetroot, scrambled egg and bread. In the glimmering half-light they made no sound – apart from the scrape of cutlery on plates – and sat three or four feet away from one another.

Many were old, grey and balding; some had ruddy faces and others were pasty with more than a few being young men, short of hair and with bright, animated movements. A man in a small, brick pulpit – according to the Benedictine rule – read a book as they ate. The reading was slow and incantatory. Tonight it was the story of Orione, a man who had just been beatified.

They ate fast since they didn't want to keep anyone else waiting. First and last this was a community of men in which sensitivity to one another was finely honed. Yet the brevity and simplicity of the meals were very much a part of the lifestyle of Quarr – perhaps the most simple and unadorned life to be found anywhere in Britain.

After a short period of recreation more bells heralded the start of Compline or evening prayer. Within these walls bells were the music of the nights and days. They struck off the hours and announced the beginning and end of prayers. We heard tiny tinkling bells, fat, echoing bells and huge romping gongs which bounced right down to the very foundations of the crypt.

I had come by train to Portsmouth, crossing on the ferry to Ryde where I took a taxi to this strange place and had been welcomed by these pained, unworldly men who were afraid of cameras, unwilling to look you directly in the eye and only spoke when spoken to and then with a great deal of effort.

Compline was a sight of religious beauty, stirring the spirit and the eye. The robed monks took their places in the choir stalls and almost immediately the lights were turned out with but one burning candle. As they chanted and knelt before God, their black, rounded shapes revolved around and dissolved into one another in the flickering light. Their voices, amplified by the empty nave, were astonishingly strong as the Gregorian chants carolled out, sometimes in unison and sometimes duelling as the sacred mysteries were celebrated. Finally the Abbot sprinkled holy water over all as a purification. Catch a drop on your cheek and it seemed to burn.

At nine came The Great Night Silence when all that could be heard was the wind hurtling around the monastery walls and shaking the branches of the pine trees in the gardens. *May the Lord grant us a quiet night and a perfect end.*

Even in the night silence there were still tiny bells ringing soft and sweet, redolent with the jubilation of Christmas carols. And the wind kept sighing in the pines until, at 5am, the cloister bells pealed out again, fat and assertive, stirring the monks out of their slumbers in readiness for Matins, which is the only service of the day in which they don their hoods.

This is the coldest time of day and the Benedictine tradition holds that a donned hood reinforces the desired feeling of isolation and oneness with God alone. It is a service of psalms, hymns and scripture reading.

In the half an hour between Matins and Lauds, Dom Matthew Taylor has a period of silent prayer in his room. The monastic life, he told me, was one long process of coming close to God. 'Yet the closer you come, the further away God seems to be. He is nothing like his created reality. The more you understand the more you realise you don't understand. He is only like himself.'

Jersey

Margaret Brockley vividly recounts her childhood memories of the time when her island was transformed into a death camp.

Their Eyes Looked Dead

Margaret Brockley

I was born in Jersey in 1935 and it was my 6th birthday when the Germans jackbooted into Jersey in July 1941.

We had been told the Germans were coming. We had had leaflets dropped but we didn't really believe it. We were sitting having our Sunday lunch when we heard the sound of planes. I ran upstairs to the bedroom and looked out. I could see what seemed like hundreds of silver fish glistening in the sky. I called my Mother to come and look. She said she didn't know whether they were ours or German.

At the time we were living not far from the docks. We had just started eating when a plane swooped down and started machine gunning. My Mother cried out 'under the table', and there we stayed with our meal getting cold until the planes had gone.

Our neighbour, who lived in the same row of cottages, came to tell us after the planes had left, that he had seen his mate blown up under one of the lorries down at the docks.

It wasn't long before another group of planes came over. This time they dropped more leaflets stating the terms they were coming on. If we didn't comply they would bomb and strafe again. The leaflets said every house in the Island must display a white flag by a certain time.

We went up the steps by the cottages and there watched people putting out bits of white cloth from their windows. The street was festooned with what was supposed to be white flags but you have never seen such insults in your life. Dirty knickers, dirty nappies, old bits of cloth, anything people could find to insult them.

When they finally arrived they had to walk up through that.

I said to my Mother... 'How long are they going to stay?' She said... 'Oh! ninety days, there's a good Geneva convention, this is an open city, the Militia and the troops have left, there's nobody armed here, they should be out in ninety days.' But they stayed right through the war.

*   *   *

One day I heard my Mother talking about a neighbour. We had not seen him for days then news came that he was part of a forced labour group recently formed. This was a new innovation evidently brought in to boost slave labour which we knew they had been using.

I was down near the docks. There were barricades of barbed wire and trestles and two sentries.

We could look across to where the weighbridge was and only one sentry. My brother and I had been watching all morning the coming and going from the boats. We couldn't get down to the dock but we could see quite well from where we had climbed. About fifty yards back there was another barricade. No one was allowed beyond that but we'd passed the one and they hadn't stopped us, so we pressed on. They seemed not to bother as we were children. One of the things they used to say was 'Rause kleine kinden' (clear off young children) but we didn't take any notice. This particular sentry must have seen us but he didn't take any notice and went to the other end of the barricade. He just turned his back on us, and left us there.

From off one of the ships I saw something that stays with me to this day. It horrified me so deeply. It was terrible. There must have been about 30 people came from one of the ships. I found out later they were Russians. There were all kinds of people. There were men, there were women, and there were small children some the same age as me. They were all in rags. They looked terribly tired and their feet were the things that I looked at. We used to run barefoot a lot of the time but their feet were wrapped up in rags soaked with blood and cake dried blood where they had been made to walk. Their clothes hung about them and they looked utterly drained. Their eyes looked dead and there was one old man being pushed and shoved along. He must have been 80ish but looked more. He had white hair and a white beard like old Father Time. To my childish mind it seemed the longest beard I'd ever seen. His arm was around a child he was trying to shield from the Nazis who were whipping these poor souls trying to make them walk faster. All they could do was shuffle along and I saw one woman fall. The Nazi guard just pushed her out of the way with his boot. It seemed they were made to walk miles to the camp near the tunnels which they had begun to dig out.

When they were too ill to work they were pushed over the cliff, onto a small bay and lime was poured down there. There were hundreds pushed over the cliff but at the end of the war I don't think there was much left of them, they continually poured lime on and burned them. The only way we could find out about any of these things was from the locals who were forced labour.

My Mother was in the 'underground information' and from time to time the man who had worked in the tunnels, our neighbour, told her this particular group had been fed, allowed to sleep until the next day and then been made to work ... all of them, men, women, and children. Whole families had arrived but they didn't last long, they had suffered so much, they had been starved and beaten and they died quickly. It seems no one knows where they put the bodies.

Those sights and those stories have stayed with me all my life... a nightmare which returns from time to time... I shudder when I think what must it have been like for those who were actually in the concentration and death camps.

I suppose I was about nine when all that happened but as I'm talking it seems like yesterday.

Scillies

The late novelist, John Fowles had a great love for islands, in general, and for the Scillies, in particular. Whether or not one is convinced by his theory as to the origin of the enduring myth of Atlantis, Fowles is surely right in asserting that islands do 'not belong to any legal owner, but offer to become a part of all who tread and love them'.

Forever Just Out Of Reach

John Fowles

The wise visitor to the Scillies does not drive straight to Penzance and board a helicopter or a ship, but finds time, so long as the weather is clear and visibility good, to go out first to Land's End. And there they float, an eternal stone armada of over a hundred ships, aloofly anchored off England; mute, enticing, forever just out of reach. The effect is best later in the day, when they lie in the westering sun's path, more like optical illusions, mirages, than a certain reality. I say 'they', but the appearance at this range is of one island; which has a justice in it, since in remote antiquity all the larger islands except St Agnes very probably were conjoined.

At Land's End you already stand on territory haunted by much earlier mankind. Their menhirs and quoits and stone lines brood on the moors and in the granite-walled fields; and even today the Scillies can in certain lights lose the name we now call them by and re-become the Hesperidean Islands of the Blest; Avalon, Lyonesse, Glasinnis, the Land of the Shades; regain all the labels that countless centuries of Celtic folklore and myth have attached to them. Adam and Eve braved the sea, probably as long as four thousand years ago. Their burial places are scattered all over the present islands, and so densely in places that one suspects the Scillies must have been the ultimate Forest Lawn of megalithic Britain, though interment there would not have been an ambition of only the dying. The spirits of the dead could not cross water, and the living may well have cherished that thirty-mile *cordon sanitaire* between themselves and their ancestors. Whatever the reason, the islands hold an astounding concentration of nearly one-fifth of all such tombs in England and Wales – far more than Cornwall, which is already rich in them.

Some of the great boulders, naturally carved by Atlantic wind and rain, split and isolated by the Ice Age, that the earliest settlers found there would have profoundly impressed, and baffled, them. They are so splendidly wrought and monumental – especially on Gugh and the south side of St Agnes – that it is as if some earlier incarnation of Henry Moore has played a huge joke (in one case a huge phallic joke) on posterity. The pluperfect one lies on the furze-moor just above Porth Askin, exquisitely posed and pedestalled in a rainwater pool. It would grace the forecourt of any twentieth-century skyscraper: and much higher praise, not disgrace the most fastidious Zen garden. Perhaps it was these magnificent stones that seeded the legend of the lost land of Lyonesse and the associated myth of Atlantis; of a simpler, nobler, vanished world and culture.

I should have made a very poor hand on Ulysses' boat, since I have never in my life had to go by an island without wishing that I could have landed on it, and even in less than traditionally romantic circumstances. I had the longing only very recently, on a tour round Manhattan; would have had our launch stop at all those forsaken islets with their dilapidated warehouses and weed jungles. In some way they put to shame the far more famous island they surrounded, and remained of their kind, where it has become a termite-heap. True islands always play the sirens' (and bookmakers') trick: they lure by challenging, by daring. Somewhere on them one will become Crusoe again, one will discover something: the iron-bound chest, the jackpot, the outside chance. The Greek island I lived on in the early 1950s was just such a place. Like Crusoe, I never knew who I really was, what I lacked (what the psycho-analytical theorists of artistic making call the 'creative gap'), until I had wandered in its solitudes and emptinesses. Eventually it let me feel it was mine: which is the other great siren charm of islands – that they will not belong to any legal owner, but offer to become a part of all who tread and love them.

Caldey Island

David Clensy records a profound turning point in the life of one man and in the life of this unique island community.

A Moment Of High Realism

David Clensy

The problem is that there are hardly any Catholics in Wales, the Abbot explained as he pondered upon a fact that had been worrying him for some time. For Caldey Island, with its famous monastic abbey holds a contradictory place in Welsh society. It is often held up as a pinnacle of Welsh culture and history. Yet for almost thirty years its small Cistercian community has been completely devoid of any Welsh presence.

As dawn broke on the first St. David's Day of the new millennium, however, things were about to change.

For the monks that line the choir stalls the day is already hours old. They have risen in the dark of the night for their 3.30am Office of Vigils, spent a number of hours reading, praying and contemplating silently. Now as they reach the end of their second Office, Lauds, the chanted psalms trip off their tongues with the dexterous comfort that comes from lifetimes of repetition.

Watching them from a pew at the back of the church is like looking at a painting; a moment of high realism depicting the romance of medieval life. These pews stand in angular opposition to the choir stalls of the monks. They act as a place for lay-people (both men and women) to come and witness the Offices. For the handful of women that live on the island this is the nearest that they can come to entering the abbey. A piously-shawled figure is occasionally silently present. This morning they are empty, except for the pew in front of me, which is occupied by a tall, gaunt man in his mid-sixties. As he stands, his heavy overcoat protecting him from the morning chill, he follows every action, gesture and response of the monks. There is nothing in his expression of concentration however that gives away the fact that his life will alter dramatically, almost irrecoverably, within the next few hours. Yet he is perfectly aware of it, for today Michael is to join this small, isolated Cistercian community, with every intention of devoting the rest of his life to monastic austerity.

*   *   *

What could make a person want to devote himself to such an austere life? Brother Dominic, a monk for 53 years, and originally from New York, was in the US Air Force during the war. My air-force style flying-jacket brought back vivid memories for him.

It was when I saw my friends lying there, burnt and ripped-up – and saw the expression of relief on the faces of those that received Catholic Communion before dying, that I suddenly felt the calling.

I approached Brother Gildas, the unswervingly hospitable Guest Master, and asked him if tragedy was often a reason for joining the monastic community.

It's something that we have to watch very carefully for, he confided through his impressive Marxian beard, *We have to be sure that it's not just a negative response to something like that. Of course, it sometimes happens that an occurrence such as that provides the impetus for a real vocation . . . we all have our own stories.*

Back in the abbey though, the third Office of the day, Terce, was approaching fast, and with it the moment when Michael would join the community. I met him outside his room in the guest quarters, preparing to leave. I wished him good luck, and watched him as he walked into his room. He picked up the sum of his worldly possessions – a small suitcase, and an overcoat folded across his arm. In this epiphanic moment the sun emerged from behind a cloud and filled the room with tangible beams of light. Michael stopped, a resplendent silhouette against this golden wash. He took a sharp intake of breath. It was the only sign of nerves at this enormously significant, yet highly understated moment. He then stepped out of the room, and casually walked towards his new life. Almost as if for a walk in the park.

I sat for a time alone in my room as his footsteps diminished to silence. I felt incredibly honoured to have been the only witness to this life-changing moment. This tentative step across the threshold between now and forever. The old, deep rooted oak tree that stood outside my window rustled peacefully, protected from the wind by the great white-washed walls of the abbey. There was a distant sound of monastic chanting. The intricate harmonies of the choir stalls seemed all the richer for the addition of a Welsh voice.

Bardsey

Bardsey has been a place of pilgrimage since the early years of Christianity. R.S. Thomas called the island 'a great draft of Nature' and its few remaining inhabitants 'all castaways on a sea of grass'. Here, Tom Davies has a fleeting encounter with the island's hermit.

The Fair Flower Of Wales

Tom Davies

Everything about the morning was lovely. Being surrounded by water. The pleasing tidiness of the fields shorn of all spare grass by the foraging sheep and rabbits. The grey stone cottages. The snatched sounds of hymnody being born aloft and shaken around by the sun-drenched winds. Forever enchanting to the Welsh ear are such sounds which, like the smell of roast beef and the theme tune of 'Family Favourites', tell of all those plump Sundays of our childhoods when we lay around eating too much, listening to the radio as Mam washed up the dishes and worrying that, one day, she would stop loving us and run off somewhere.

I only caught the final notes of the last hymn of the service though what could be a more beautiful setting for any act of worship than this ancient rubble with the call of the birds in the rafters of a great blue sky, surrounded by, on one side, Anglesey, just here the mighty sweep of Cardigan Bay and, way over the sea, the Wicklow mountains in Ireland? The small congregation filed out through the graveyard where, on a huge Celtic cross, there was the telling inscription: 'Is it nothing to you, all ye who pass by?'

When all of them had left I introduced myself to Brother Nathanael, a Franciscan friar who said that, as soon as he had changed out of his vestments, he would take me down to his house for a cup of coffee. He was here for the summer to look after pilgrims and seemed positively abrim with the love and gaiety of his spiritual leader, St Francis.

As we were going back along the path to his house a woman came walking across a field towards us. She moved as slowly as a publisher's decision, with tiny stooped shoulders, fingers bent with arthritis and a black cowl over her head. She smiled, showing a few gold teeth below a simply enormous beak of a nose and the large, sad brown eyes of a boxer dog. 'Your visitor might like this,' she said in a voice so soft you could barely hear it as she handed Nathanael a leaflet entitled *Tramping Down Death by Death*. 'You are both well I hope.'

With this, and before we could say anything, she left us as softly and slowly as she had come. She was Sister Helen Mary, the hermit on the island. She spoke rarely and survived on a small vegetable patch and a lot of prayer, Nathanael explained. She was one of the Sisters of the Love of God and had been living in the loft of some old stables for ten years now. If Nathanael ever complained to her about anything her reply was always the same: 'Pray, brother, just pray. Nothing else matters.'

As he made the coffee, Nathanael admitted he did not know much about modern things. 'When I first came here no one had a fridge. There was no electricity, just calor gas lamps, candles or torches.' He also had the tattiest gown I have ever seen – all patches and stitches with so many rips it would have been rejected by an Oxfam shop on a slow day. 'It's my second best,' he said when I asked if the vow of poverty meant just one gown until you died. 'I was going under some barbed wire the other day and tore the sleeve here. I fear it's on its last legs now.'

We talked of the island and he smiled as he said it really was possible that 20,000 had been buried here. Wherever you dug there were masses of bones. 'Any historical journal will tell you that all along the coast right down to Aberystwyth, people always asked to be buried here. They would even have makeshift mortuaries where they stored the bodies if the weather was too bad to get over to the island.'

Nathanael was an Anglican Franciscan who tried to welcome every pilgrim to the island in the summer. At that moment he was friary-less since his last friary had been closed down, but at the end of that summer he was going to be based in Llandudno as a part-time priest. Much of his time on the island was spent in prayer: morning compline, midday office and evening prayer. Prayer, you sensed, provided him with the pattern of fidelity crucial to his love of the Lord. In a way his life was one long, secret prayer.

Being a good Franciscan he loved the profusion of birds and rabbits. He was saddened when myxomatosis struck the island and many of the rabbits had died. Only that morning he had seen one such rabbit with its face swollen up and blind, bumping wretchedly against a stone wall. Even as he spoke, his gentle radiance told me much about the practice and presence of God. He was one of those rare and valuable men who mediate the idea of God to us; a simple, good man in whom you can find the very icon of the risen Christ. We spoke for a while about another good man I knew: Canon David Watson, the great York evangelist who had recently been stricken by cancer. Then we sat around a table and prayed for David's recovery; that God would send his angels to kiss the disease out of David's body; that he would be fully restored to us and the Church.

It was one of those prayers in which we had all entered into a dialogue with the power of healing Love. When we had finished it, there was nothing more to say.

Anglesey

In his 'Autobiographies', R.S. Thomas writes of himself in the third person as if he was describing the thoughts and actions of a stranger. Here he writes of his intense childhood in a place where 'there would be always someone gazing at the sea'.

Not A Dead Thing

R.S. Thomas

What does Holyhead stand for? For the sea, of course, as it is an island, Ynys Gybi, Holy Island. Even though it is only a strip of water that makes it an island, the sea is still close enough and plays an important part in the lives of its people. There was a good harbour there, and before a storm it would fill with sailing ships of all kinds, until it was more like a forest. The sea became part of the child's life also, its noise, its smell, its ferocity on windy days. It was to be seen from his bedroom. At night the flashes from the lighthouse would dart through his room like the sails of a windmill. There would always be someone gazing at the sea, as if he were expecting something to happen. These were old sailors, their sailing days gone by. But there were also young men, waiting for their chance to go to the aid of a ship in trouble. There was a lifeboat, but the young men would be out in their small boats long before it was launched. In stormy weather, when the ship from Ireland was late, a fit of apprehension would seize the town, that wouldn't pass until the sound of the ship's horn, announcing that she had arrived safely, was heard. Sometimes his mother would see his father off, and while they stood on the quay the captain would call from the bridge, pretending to offer to take the boy with them. All this went on around the harbour and the docks, but there was another side to the island too, where there were only a few farms and scattered houses. In that area, there was one particular family, and the boy became close friends with the children. The mother was a widow, with two sons and a daughter. The house, Bryn Awel, came to mean something very special to him. He would love going there to play and sometimes to stay overnight with them. He would listen to the wind singing fiercely around the house, and first thing in the morning would slink from his bed to gaze at the white waves of the sea about a quarter of a mile away. Because he was in school by this time, there was nothing he liked better than to accompany his new friends on their way home, especially in the autumn when the sun was setting, the air chilly, and their heads full of plans for Guy Fawkes. Days in advance they would gather sticks and boxes and wood to make an enormous bonfire for old Guy. Oh, how he would look forward to that day, with its fireworks and the chance to be out in the dark, out of the sight and care of his parents. And then back to the house to have fun with the apples hanging from the rafters. And best of all, of course, the journey home under the stars, with the gorse creaking in the wind enough to turn the blood to ice, because memories of Halloween and its ghosts were still within the recall of some of the old people. To a sensitive boy, ghosts were real enough – and how else is it possible to explain something that happened later?

It was winter, and though Holyhead was quite a mild place, a pond on the mountain had frozen over, with some snow around it. The three of them were there late in the afternoon, with night beginning to fall. In the middle of the pond there was a small patch that had not frozen. Two of them were looking down from a bank, with the third out of sight somewhere behind. Suddenly a figure appeared in front of them, running towards the edge of the clear water. The two shouted simultaneously, warning the other to be careful. But the next minute he joined them from an entirely different direction, and at the same time the apparition disappeared. The two would have been willing to agree that it was a dream, were it not for the fact that both of them had shouted simultaneously.

His parents would sometimes want to go out of an evening. 'Will you be all right on your own?' Of course he would. He hated admitting anything different. After they had gone, silence would take possession of the house. Slowly, he would realise that he was on his own. And yet, was he? A house is not a dead thing. It is given to sighing, squeaking and whispering. He would listen. Wasn't there someone upstairs? What was that noise, as of a man breathing? He would go to the bottom of the stairs and turn on the light. And yet the far end of the upstairs was in shadow. He would shout. No answer. He would climb the stairs, step by step, and having reached the top would listen again. Suddenly he would leap forward a step or two, thundering with his feet and shouting: 'Boo!' Nothing. No-one. He would come downstairs with some relief, and begin reading again in front of the fire until his parents came home.

A man's personality is a strange thing. It reveals itself in mysterious ways. From where did the boy get the idea of making an effigy, dressing it and placing it on a chair at the head of the stairs? And when his parents came in, there was the figure waiting for them in the shadows. And of course it was his mother who was the first to climb the stairs and have the shock of her life. Then screams and a great commotion, and his father reading him the riot act for such foolishness. And yet it was all quite innocent. They would have gladly stayed at home, were it not for the fact that he had assured them that he would be all right.

Skellig Michael

*Geoffrey Grigson sets foot on this pinnacle of rock which was once home to centuries
of Irish monks who had sought and found this ultimate desert in the ocean.*

Hard Devotion

Geoffrey Grigson

It was extraordinary to be out and up on this rock, this maritime
mountain, this Michael's Mount, where under the proper protection of St
Michael the Archangel, the Irish monks had reproduced the religious aus-
terities of the Egyptian desert. Enough is known of Irish monasticism to
be sure of how they lived their penitential life as a *militia Christi* on Skellig
Michael. The details you can find in Father Ryan's *Irish Monasticism*. They
watched and prayed and worked in self-mortification. They prayed before
dawn by candlelight, and again at sunset, and after a little sleep again at
midnight when they were woken up for the night vigil, the *nocturnae solem-
nitates*. The asceticism of labour was enjoined for them under the
Pachomian Rule: they could neither talk nor laugh at work; rather they
must pray, meditate, and chant the psalms. On Skellig Michael, on the precipitous slopes (which drop away to the Atlantic from the cashel walls),
you might think there was little opportunity for the gardening and the
corn-growing of Irish monasteries. But there was, no doubt, a garden
within the walls, and though it is now much eroded, corn may have been
grown on the soil of Christ's Saddle between the two peaks. An eighteenth century historian of Kerry maintained that Christ's Saddle had
been cultivated and that ridges of the plots where corn had been grown
were visible then inside the cashel. Vegetables, flour and water and bread
were the chief items of the austere diet of Celtic monasticism, but in spite
of the Pachomian Rule, flesh seems to have been allowed. In St
Columba's monastery on the Scottish island of Iona, they ate oxen, sheep,
seals and fish. On Skellig they could have had the seals and the fish, and

they perhaps ate the puffins which breed on the island, as well as gannets from Little Skellig.

I was doubtful at first whether the steps and the stone paths were as old as the monastery, the buildings of which would go back, as I say, at least to the eighth or seventh century. Long after the monastery had been deserted and up to the eighteenth century, Skellig Michael was an island to which pilgrims came and followed a journey of the Stations of the Cross, which ended on the high peak where the pilgrims, one by one, squeezed out through a cleft called the Needles' Eye and reached to a rock hanging over the Atlantic on which a cross is engraved. The steps cover the island, go up and down and round and across the precipices. Here and there a landfall has carried them away, here and there they vanish under sea-pink. I thought they might belong to the later centuries of pilgrimage, but the monks certainly built stone paths in other monasteries, and I suspect that building them on Skellig and keeping them in order were skilful and dangerous parts of that labour by which they mortified their bodies.

Of these Irish soldiers of Christ, living in a discipline severe beyond that of any army, we know at least one thing unprovided for in the rule St Pachomius laid down. We know they wrote poems, or that some of them wrote poems; and these poems embody a clean-swept vision of delight in their calling, their religion, and the natural order created by the God they worshipped. One of these poems, a late one, though it was supposed to have been written by St Columba or Collum Cille, applies so much to Skellig Michael that you should search it out among the fine translations in Kenneth Jackson's *Early Celtic Nature Poetry*. I shall leave that to you, and say a little of the slender history of Skellig Michael.

It is not possible to tell exactly when the monastery was founded or by whom. The bay across from the Skelligs is called St Finnian's Bay, and the foundation has been given, though not, I think, with much authority, to St Finnian, the great 'tutor of the saints of Ireland', the instructor of St Brendan the Navigator and of St Columba. Finnian died in 549. The monastery may indeed have been founded by him or by one of his disciples. Finnian deepened and advanced the monastic life and made it more strict, and his disciples founded a good many island monasteries in which the life of contemplation was still further removed from the distractions and divisions of men. About 822, according to a story repeated in various annals, the Vikings raided Skellig Michael, climbed the steps into the cloud, and took off with them a monk named Edgall, but Skellig was not yet deserted and there are records in the *Annals of the Four Masters* of the death of monks or abbots on Skellig in 950 and 1044. Perhaps the monastery was occupied up to the Anglo-Norman seizure and settlement of Ireland, perhaps till later. It is still venerated. Stories about it are still current. Our boatmen told us, as Skellig was beginning to fade back to blue on the horizon, of the man who had taken water from one of the two wells within the cashel walls and how the water would not boil in his kettle. He told us – which is true enough – that the gannets from Little Skellig never settle on Skellig Michael; and in Charles Smith's *State of the County of Kerry*, published in 1756, you will find a story that 'no bird hath the power to fly over that part of it where the chapels and walls stand, without first alighting on the ground, which they walk gently over, and then take wing'.

I spent most of a day on Skellig Michael and came away reluctantly enough. Militant Protestants have had much to say of the selfishness and defeatism of the monastic life. I don't know. I am neither Protestant, except by upbringing, nor Catholic, but is it not moving to a degree, and not merely to a romantic degree, when we think of that withdrawn life in the wilderness of islands, off these Irish coasts, off Scotland, off Wales, off Brittany, in the Isles of Scilly, in the Farne Islands, and far up in the north in the Westmann Islands, off Iceland? When we think of the quiet of that selfless and hard devotion to an end which is superhuman? Moving about the coasts of Kerry afterwards, I understood what a symbol Skellig Michael must have been to those who were neither monks nor clergy, seeing it on the horizon, a single or a double peak, but always blue, always or often, with its nimbus of white cloud, its trailing coif of holiness.

Great Blaskets

Perhaps no other group of islands in Britain and Ireland have produced more fine native writers in the 20th century than the Great Blaskets and here, one of the finest, Peig Sayers bids a moving farewell to this 'little rose in the wilderness'.

The Last Chapter

Peig Sayers

My spell on this little bench is nearly finished. It's sad and low and lonely I am to be parting with it. Long as the day is, night comes, and alas, the night is coming for me, too.

I am parting with you, beautiful little place, sun of my life. Other people will have your pleasure in future, but I'll be far away from you in a kingdom I don't know. Big Peig, as the children call me, will be there no more, but maybe a better woman would. But she won't have as much pleasure as I had, because great as was my sorrow and heart torment, God of Glory and His Blessed Mother helped me. I was often standing here studying the works of the Creator and tasting His royal sweetness in my heart. Everything He created was a consolation to me, even unto the grief itself, it would make me think deeper. I thought there was nothing in the things of this life but poverty – this place full today and empty tomorrow – hadn't I got it to be seen, clearly. The people I knew in my youth, it was often they had the stone in the gauntlet for each other. They were strong, courageous, strong worded, but they all fell, they were cleared out of the world. It was the same do the people who were there before them got, and may God have mercy on us, where is their work today? Other people to be in their place, without the slightest thought for them. I think everything is folly except for loving God!

I am now at tight grips with the years, and many a thing I saw. Everything I was interested in I didn't let it astray. Someone else will have pastime out of my work when I'm gone on the way of truth. A person here and a person there will say, maybe, 'Who was that Peig Sayers' but poor Peig will be the length of their shout from them. This green bench where she used to do the studying will be a domicile for the birds of the wilderness, and the little house where she used to eat and drink, it's unlikely there'll be a trace of it there.

These thoughts appearing in my heart today are lonely. They are not pleasant for me but I can't help them. Here they are towards me in their thousands; they are like soldiers. As I scatter them, they come together again. It's no good for me to be at them. They have beaten me. My blessing and the blessing of God be with Youth; and my advice to everyone is to borrow from this life, because a spool is no faster turning than it. My life is spent, as a candle, and my hope is up every day that I'll be called into the eternal kingdom.

O God who is in Heaven, my trust and my hope is fully in you! May you guide me on this long road I have not travelled before! It's often during my life you helped me. Well I know your holy help, because I was often held by sorrow, with no escape. When the need was highest, it was then you would lay your merciful eye on me, and a light like the shining of the sun would come on my worried mind. The clouds of sorrow would be gone without trace; in place there would be some spiritual joy whose sweetness I cannot describe here.

But I have this much to say, that I had good neighbours. We helped each other and lived in the shelter of each other. Everything that was coming dark upon us, we would disclose it to each other, and that would give us consolation of mind. Friendship was the fastest root in our hearts.

It was like a little rose in the wilderness I grew up; without for company only those gems that God of Glory created, eternal praise to Him! Every early morning in the summer when the sun would show its face up over the top of Eagle Mountain I was often looking at it and at the same time making wonder of the colours in the sky around us. I remember well that there used to be little yellow, golden rays as slender roads coming to me from the top of the mountain, and that the mountain used to be red and a big belt of every colour, between white, yellow and black, around the sky and every colour giving its own appearance on the great, wet sea. I think, there was welcome in the heart of every creature for the sparkling of the morning.

There are people and they think that this island is a lonely, airy place. That is true for them, but the peace of the Lord is in it. I am living in it for more than forty years, and I didn't see two of the neighbours fighting in it yet. It was like honey for my poor tormented heart to rise up on the shoulder of the mountain footing the turf or gathering the sods on each other. Very often I'd throw myself back in the green heather, resting. It wasn't for bone-laziness I'd do it, but for the beauty of the hills and the rumble of the waves that would be grieving down from me, in dark caves where the seals of the sea lived – those and the blue sky without a cloud travelling it, over me – it was those made me do it, because those were the pictures most pleasant to my heart, and it's those I was most used to.

A person would say, maybe, that it was a simple life we were living, but nobody would say that our life was comfortable. Our own hardships followed us. It's often we were in a way to go with fear and fright, because when winter came it wasn't its habit to come gentle and kind. The great sea was coming on top of us and the strong force of the wind helping it. We had but to send our prayer sincerely to God that nobody would be taken sick or ill. We had our own charge of that because there wasn't a priest or doctor near us without going across the little strait and the little strait was up to three miles in length. But God was in favour with us, eternal praise to Him! For with my memory nobody died without the priest in winter-time.

Farewell to the things of this life now, and especially to the pleasant, gay time I have spent here. I'm afraid I'll do no more work in future for the language of the superior men, but I have done a person's share, maybe. I would do as much more, and have the heart for it, but the time is spent.

Pray for me, friends and dear people, that God will give me help for the long road!

Aran Islands

The great novelist and short story writer, Liam O' Flaherty returns to the island of his birth for solace but he fails to regain the 'promised land' he'd left behind.

An Alien Returns

Liam O'Flaherty

Now I remembered how I went back there after the publication of my novel, *The Black Soul,* had persuaded me that I could never hope to carry the fortress of literature by assault. That was the song with which I hoped to storm the highest heavens, but it was received instead by a storm of the most violently adverse criticism. Edward Garnett wrote to me saying that the critics had killed the book for ten years. I felt that they had killed me with it, and my childish vanity drove me into a frenzy of rage. I wrote to him saying that these critics did not have sufficient blood in them to contract syphilis, and then I got on the train for the Aran Islands, swearing that I would never leave it again.

In Galway I met my sister. At that time she was very ill, but in my excitement at returning home I did not notice it. On the boat coming from Galway to the islands, she told me how difficult things were for her at home, how father was alone and doting. Whose father? What? I walked up and down the deck of the boat, crying out as each headland came into view. When the grey mass of the islands rose suddenly from the white-capped sea, I felt that this was indeed the promised land to which I had returned. All the people on the boat looked askance at me, for I had already become a damned soul in their eyes. But I was indifferent to them also and I stood apart, opening my mouth, so that the wild sea wind could rush freely into my lungs, to blow away the rank air of cities. And then we reached the shore.

Immediately, I felt an alien among the people who stood on the pier. They spoke to me and shook me by the hand, but there was fear in their eyes. Had it been hatred, I would not have felt an alien; but this mute fear was deeper than hatred and unapproachable. One could not speak to it, haul it out from the soul and hold it up for examination. It was like a shameful vice which one does not acknowledge even to one's conscience. I walked up the pier with my sister, glancing shyly, with a timid lover's eyes, at the familiar rocks, fields, houses and at the same time feeling all round me these watching eyes and the whispered pity for one who had been a kinsman and had become contaminated. With what?

The madness of prophecy, no less. This is the greatest sin in the eyes of the herd. And when one of the herd becomes gifted with this madness, he at once becomes an object of fear for the rest. In strong and rich societies he is tolerated as an amusing outcast; but in a weak and poor herd, the fear is much greater, sometimes leading to expulsion and death. A criminal! To sing of beauty should be such a lovely thing.

Even my sister had the same fear in her eyes, but she was too near my blood to show it; and I, even though I felt that fear, was too exalted to be affected by it on the surface. Yet I was glad when we got to the hotel and were alone. And then we walked west to see my father. It was an afternoon in March and Spring was already in the air. The earth was turning green. It imparted its fever to me. And yet, I could not enjoy this fever because of my sister who gave it a different meaning. To her it was a manifestation of God's bounty showing His love for men, softening their hearts and making them repent of their sins, in order to win a place in Paradise, where they could sing of beauty for all eternity. But I wanted to sing then, at that very moment; to seize the people who passed by the bosom and shout at them: "Come, brothers and sisters, listen to the call of Spring and make merry while the blood is still warm in your veins. Soon the day will come when your blood will cease to flow and worms shall devour your flesh, which can now feel the delights of tender passion".

And then, seeing that even my sister whom I loved had become alien to me, I knew that it was no use my fleeing to this island that had given me birth. These people were even more hostile to me than the critics who had denounced my book. They were all, both the critics and these people among whom I was born, of the common herd, slaveling serfs who grovelled before false gods; gods in their own liking; toy monsters without any noble attribute. A pride like Lucifer's buoyed me up to the sombre loneliness of universal understanding; the pride of Socrates when the hemlock moistened his doomed tongue and his wit was martyred by the envious mob of Athens. "Father, forgive them for they know not what they do." Forgive them not, I say, but lash their slavish backs and make them minister unto your wants. Wherever you see an ignorant eye spit on it; for it has committed the sin against the Holy Ghost by looking into yours, its master's eye.

It was already dusk when we came to our village. With horror I saw the house where I was born, falling rapidly into ruins. The little garden in front was overgrown with weeds. The roof of the outhouse was sagging in the middle. Grass was growing through the thatch. And within the house itself there was the same air of desolation. But more desolate than the house and its surroundings was my father himself, that doddering old man who shook hands with me and mumbled half articulate words without knowing me.

John Millington Synge recounts the islanders' extraordinary death rituals which helped them to overcome the 'terror of the world'.

The Ecstacy of Grief

J. M. Synge

After Mass this morning an old woman was buried. She lived in the cottage next mine, and more than once before noon I heard a faint echo of the keen. I did not go to the wake for fear my presence might jar upon the mourners, but all last evening I could hear the strokes of a hammer in the yard, where, in the middle of a little crowd of idlers, the next of kin laboured slowly at the coffin. Today, before the hour for the funeral, poteen was served to a number of men who stood about upon the road, and a portion was brought to me in my room. Then the coffin was carried out sewn loosely in sailcloth, and held near the ground by three crosspoles lashed upon the top. As we moved down to the low eastern portion of the island, nearly all the men, and all the oldest women, wearing petticoats over their hands, came out and joined in the procession.

While the grave was being opened the women sat down among the flat tombstones, bordered with a pale fringe of early bracken, and began the wild keen, or crying for the dead. Each old woman, as she took her turn in the leading recitative, seemed possessed for the moment with a profound ecstasy of grief, swaying to and fro, and bending her forehead to the stone before her, while she called out to the dead with a perpetually recurring chant of sobs.

All round the graveyard other wrinkled women, looking out from under the deep red petticoats that cloaked them, rocked themselves with the same rhythm, and intoned the inarticulate chant that is sustained by all as an accompaniment.

The morning had been beautifully fine, but as they lowered the coffin into the grave, thunder rumbled overhead and hailstones hissed among the bracken.

In Inishmaan one is forced to believe in a sympathy between man and nature, and at this moment when the thunder sounded a death-peal of extraordinary grandeur above the voices of the women, I could see the faces near me stiff and drawn with emotion.

This grief of the keen is no personal complaint for the death of one woman over eighty years, but seems to contain the whole passionate rage that lurks somewhere in every native of the island. In this cry of pain the inner consciousness of the people seems to lay itself bare for an instant, and to reveal the mood of beings who feel their isolation in the face of a universe that wars on them with winds and seas. They are usually silent, but in the presence of death all outward show of indifference or patience is forgotten, and they shriek with pitiable despair before the horror of the fate to which they all are doomed.

Before they covered the coffin an old man kneeled down by the grave and repeated a simple prayer for the dead. There was an irony in these words of atonement and Catholic belief spoken by voices that were still hoarse with the cries of pagan desperation.

A little beyond the grave I saw a line of old women who had recited in the keen sitting in the shadow of a wall beside the roofless shell of the church. They were still sobbing and shaken with grief, yet they were beginning to talk again of the daily trifles that veil for them the terror of the world.

W.B. Yeats writes with astonishing insight on the profound influence which life on the Aran Islands — 'where there is neither riches or poverty' — had on his friend, John Millington Synge.

The Weight Of Necessity

W. B. Yeats

'When I got up this morning,' he writes, after he had been a long time in Inishmaan, 'I found that the people had gone to Mass and latched the kitchen door from the outside, so that I could not open it to give myself light.'

'I sat for nearly an hour beside the fire with a curious feeling that I should be quite alone in this little cottage. I am so used to sitting here with the people that I have never felt the room before as a place where any man might live and work by himself. After a while as I waited, with just light enough from the chimney to let me see the rafters and the greyness of the walls, I became indescribably mournful, for I felt that this little corner on the face of the world, and the people who live in it, have a peace and dignity from which we are shut for ever.'

This life, which he describes elsewhere as the most primitive left in Europe, satisfied some necessity of his nature. Before I met him in Paris he had wandered over much of Europe, listening to stories in the Black Forest, making friends with servants and with poor people, and this from an aesthetic interest, for he had gathered no statistics, had no money to give, and cared nothing for the wrongs of the poor, being content to pay for the pleasure of eye and ear with a tune upon the fiddle. He did not love them the better because they were poor and miserable, and it was only when he found Inishmaan and the Blaskets, where there is neither riches nor poverty, neither what he calls 'the nullity of the rich' nor 'the squalor of the poor,' that his writing lost its old morbid brooding, that he found his genius and his peace. Here were men and women who under the weight of their necessity lived, as the artist lives, in the presence of death and childhood, and the great affections and the orgiastic moment when life outleaps its limits, and who, as it is always with those who have refused or escaped the trivial and the temporary, had dignity and good manners where manners mattered. Here above all was silence from all our great orator took delight in, from formidable men, from moral indignation, from the 'sciolist' who 'is never sad,' from all in modern life that would destroy the arts; and here, to take a thought from another playwright of our school, he could love time as only women and great artists do and need never sell it.

As I read *The Islands* right through for the first time since he showed it me in manuscript, I come to understand how much knowledge of the real life of Ireland went to the creation of a world which is yet as fantastic as the Spain of Cervantes. Here is the story of *The Playboy*, of *The Shadow of the Glen;* here is the ghost on horseback and the finding of the young man's body of *Riders to the Sea,* numberless ways of speech and vehement pictures that had seemed to owe nothing to observation, and all to some overflowing of himself, or to some mere necessity of dramatic construction. I had thought the violent quarrels of *The Well of the Saints* came from his love of bitter condiments, but here is a couple that quarrel all day long amid neighbours who gather as for a play. I had defended the burning of Christy Mahon's leg on the ground that an artist need but make his characters self-consistent, and yet that too was observation, for 'although these people are kindly towards each other and their children, they have no sympathy for the suffering of animals, and little sympathy for pain when the person who feels it is not in danger.' I had thought it was in the wantonness of fancy Martin Doul accused the smith of plucking his living ducks, but a few lines farther on, in this book where moral indignation is unknown, I read, 'Sometimes when I go into a cottage, I find all the women of the place down on their knees plucking the feathers from live ducks and geese.'

He loves all that has edge, all that is salt in the mouth, all that is rough to the hand, all that heightens the emotions by contest, all that stings into life the sense of tragedy; and in this book, unlike the plays where nearness to his audience moves him to mischief, he shows it without thought of other taste than his. It is so constant, it is all set out so simply, so naturally, that it suggests a correspondence between a lasting mood of the soul and this life that shares the harshness of rocks and wind. The food of the spiritual-minded is sweet, an *Indian* scripture says, but passionate minds love bitter food. Yet he is no indifferent observer, but is certainly kind and sympathetic to all about him. When an old and ailing man, dreading the coming winter, cries at his leaving, not thinking to see him again, and he notices that the old man's mitten has a hole in it where the palm is accustomed to the stick, one knows that it is with eyes full of interested affection as befits a simple man and not in the curiosity of study. When he had left the Blaskets for the last time, he travelled with a lame pensioner who had drifted there, why Heaven knows, and one morning having missed him from the inn where they were staying, he believed he had gone back to the island, and searched everywhere and questioned everybody, till he understood of a sudden that he was jealous as though the island were a woman.

High Island

The poet, Richard Murphy owned this island for many years and spent much time alone minutely observing his loved piece of land with its intricate webs of connection.

The Meaning Of A Stone

Richard Murphy

My next visits to High Island were alone, and there I wrote continuously, sometimes in the dark, with nowhere to sleep except on the ground. A notebook records my experience on three consecutive days and one night.

5.30pm., 3 August 1970, High Island, at the hermitage.

The Seal Rock and the Gull Rock lie beyond the hermitage in the south-west corner of the island . . . in flood tide the avalanche of a wave's downfall is overwhelmed by the rising force of a stronger wave surging over the rock . . . rock pipits perched on the cliff are intimately quiet . . . an isolated cormorant looks backwards over his wings, regarding the flood tide's approach, into which it will soon be forced to dive . . . seagulls on a jagged promontory stand to attention like sentinels in black and white uniforms, now and then shouting at an intruder Sieg Heil.

Perspective of stones . . . a stone altar seen through the door of the oratory . . . a sign of order surviving in ruin, of an idea outliving not only the builder but the building by which his idea was expressed . . . the cross I took from the well, fearing it might have been stolen and never recovered, meant less when I stood it in a flower bed in my garden, where it became an ornament . . . planted beside the well where it was designed to stand, it joins a metaphysical idea to the ground . . . showing a circle within a circle on the cross, also a sun and a moon . . . on the back, limbs that end in horns, or are they water-diviner's rods or symbols handed down from the Druids?

The sun is breaking through at last, over my shoulder to the west. . . a glorious evening spreading in from the ocean after a day of heavy low-lying rain clouds . . . and at once three rabbits run out of their burrows to play . . . they are not fearless, but less afraid of us here than on the mainland . . . one rabbit has done more excavating of the abbot's clochan, another is living in the oratory, and several in the souterrain.

Between the crags of a great cliff towering on my right, I can see in the distance Shark Head and the Kimmeen Rocks. Below me a bowl of grass, richly fertilized by barnacle geese that graze there in winter, holds the peaty water of a lake used by the hermits as a millpond. Gulls are floating near the rocky verge beside the ruins of the hermitage at the centre of three circles of walls that have collapsed. Rugged outcrops of mica schist sparkle with garnetiferous quartz. Whoever named the sea-rose 'thrift' must not have noticed its improvident wild habits on High Island, its cushioning of sharp stones, and generous provision of comfortable seats. The gulls remain forever awake, watchful and sounding alarms on the bowl's perimeter, silhouetted against the evening sky.

4 August 1970, New Forge
Everything on the island connects, that is its glory, connecting what appears to be disconnected . . . the only land you can clearly see from the hermitage is Shark Head to the north and Slyne Head to the south, two ultimate fragments broken off the landmass of Europe and almost uninhabitable, the one deserted ten years ago, the other occupied by lighthouse keepers . . . but on the eastern side of the hill in the centre of the island you can see a panorama of mountains, bays, villages, islands, and rocks that lie between Achill Island and Slyne Head . . . signs of human activity on the mainland with which you cannot connect can make you yearn to get home, but looking from the hermitage out to sea, you can feel connected to the universe sublimely.

5.20pm., 5 August 1970, High Island.
I'm sitting on a rock above the blessed well, and a gentle breeze from the north is cooling the day's excessive heat . . . men are hauling lobster pots in a boat near the Seal's Rock . . . on landing I tried to cut a foothold

in the rock by striking a few blows with a sledgehammer, but the dark rock remained firm . . . an oystercatcher screeched . . . fulmar petrels, which resembled on their nests white crockery on the dresser of the cliff, took off and flew silently round and round the cove in figures of eight . . . as the tide had almost reached low water, I rowed to the cave that Emily and I had not been able to penetrate.

Inside, the vault was embossed with jade, opal, lapis lazuli and carnelian sea squirts, urchins and anemones . . . I shipped my oars and touched the walls to enter . . . a cormorant dived into the sea, leaving two young birds on a nest . . . a swell overtook me, surging into the cave, making me fear I'd be trapped . . . a wave dashed across the shingle and rumbled deep within the body of the island under its highest point before withdrawing . . . two seals were lying quite close to me on a rock, one, a spotted white cow was asleep, but the bull watched me eye to eye . . . suddenly they both dived into the water and swam under the dinghy out into the open sea . . . when I left the cave the bull followed me to the landing cove, seeing me off.

Tonight I'll keep a vigil in the holy circle of the hermitage to celebrate the feast of St Gormgall and the hatching of storm petrels in his and his hermits' graves. I feel more affection for everyone when I'm alone on High Island than when I'm among a crowd. Love, the supreme good, the redeeming harmony in every person, in all of nature, needs detachment and space as well as intimacy. Simply by being alone in this place at this time I feel its force.

Inishbofin

The American poet, Deborah Tall returns to the island in which she lived and grew to love and finds that many of the islanders have now been ensnared by the 'economic tyranny of the world of conveniences' she had sought to escape.

A Part Of What's Passing

Deborah Tall

In the older people I watch the remains of a great tradition, a resourcefulness older than Grania Uaile. And I cling to the colors and rituals of that tradition because it's given me so much faith and pleasure, and because I hope the young here won't have to grow up with the crassness and wishy-washy conformities I was reared on.

The children are wild about television. One household has bought a set which it runs off car batteries, the batteries periodically recharged off Richard and Catherine's generator. The children flock to this house every evening their parents will let them flee homework and chores to watch *Kojak* and *Rhoda* and *Hawaii Five-O*. They don't understand the accents or the jokes or the world these characters live in, but they begin to use them as a standard of life and of entertainment. Will they ever be content to stay on the island? Children I meet try to impress me with the extent of their knowledge of things American and look hungrily for more. "Is it true, Deba, in New York that people get kilt every day, more people than in Belfast altogether? That's what the schoolmaster said, but shur what does he know, he was never in it himself like ye were." I tell them it's true. "Then why would anyone want to live there a'tall?" A good question. I tell them that's why I'm living here. "Shur, there's nothin' to do here," they shrug.

So many signs of modern life have shown up since we arrived five years ago. At least ten cars and a number of tractors and dumpers now navigate the stony roads. The island had its first traffic accident, fortunately minor. There's more prosperity in evidence, more stylishness. There was even, ludicrously, a Tupperware party the other night! I couldn't believe my ears when Bridget said she hoped I'd be there. A representative from the mainland came in to explain the wonders of air-tight plastic and all the women gazed at me, a veteran of plastic, for a signal – would I support the flag, lead the way with purchases? Reluctantly, with moldy bread in mind, and their lust for progress pressing me, I did. The women cooed and committed themselves to pounds' worth; by the next week the island's bread was being stored in big rectangular plastic boxes instead of in tea towels in the dresser and everyone was singing anthems to plastic. We can't figure out where they get the money for it all, even with the increases in the dole and enlarged agricultural grants. Many of them have surpassed us in comforts, and we feel somewhat left behind by this little boom propelling the island toward the late twentieth century. We're poor even by island standards now.

Though I mourn these changes, I'm more understanding of them than before. Knowing hardship as they do, aren't they right to eliminate it wherever they can? They can't be blamed for wanting washing machines and freezers. They'll leave and get them elsewhere if they can't get them here. But I'm too keenly aware of the economic tyranny of the world of conveniences, which I feel such freedom in the absence of, and which they feel so deprived, lacking. I worry how much the island must change in order to survive, remain populated.

I live here and try to become a part of what's passing. I move backward as they move forward. My every act is a choice, a contribution toward the large weft I want to see strengthened, the fabric of island culture I hope will hold despite their self-destructive wishes.

Achill

The great German novelist, Heinrich Böll had a great love for Ireland and for Achill Island, in particular. Here he meditates on the element which pervades life in so many of our west coast islands.

Thoughts On Irish Rain

Heinrich Böll

The rain here is absolute, magnificent, and frightening. To call this rain bad weather is as inappropriate as to call scorching sunshine fine weather.

You can call this rain bad weather, but it is not. It is simply weather, and weather means rough weather. It reminds us forcibly that its element is water, falling water. And water is hard. During the war I once watched a burning aircraft going down on the Atlantic coast; the pilot landed it on the beach and fled from the exploding machine. Later I asked him why he hadn't landed the burning plane on the water, and he replied: "Because water is harder than sand."

I never believed him, but now I understood: water is hard.

And how much water can collect over three thousand miles of ocean, water that rejoices in at last reaching people, houses, terra firma, after having fallen only into water, only into itself. How can rain enjoy always falling into water?

When the electric light goes out, when the first tongue of a puddle licks its way under the door, silent and smooth, gleaming in the firelight; when the toys which the children have left lying around, when corks and bits of wood suddenly start floating and are borne forward by the tongue, when the children come downstairs, scared, and huddle in front of the fire (more surprised than scared, for they also sense the joy in this meeting of wind and rain and that this howling is a howl of delight), then we know we would not have been as worthy of the ark as Noah was. . .

Inlander's madness, to open the door to see what's up outside. Everything's up: the roof tiles, the roof gutters, even the house walls, do not inspire much confidence (for here they build temporarily, although, if they don't emigrate, they live forever in these temporary quarters – while in Europe they build for eternity without knowing whether the next generation will benefit from so much solidity).

It is a good thing always to have candles, the Bible, and a little whisky in the house, like sailors prepared for a storm; also a pack of cards, some tobacco, knitting needles and wool for the women; for the storm has a lot of breath, the rain holds a lot of water, and the night is long. Then when a second tongue of rain advances from the window and joins the first one, when the toys float slowly along the narrow tongue toward the window, it is a good thing to look up in the Bible whether the promise to send no more floods has really been given. It has been given: we can light the next candle, the next cigarette, shuffle the cards again, pour some more whisky, abandon ourselves to the drumming of the rain, the howling of the wind, the click of the knitting needles. The promise has been given.

Island More

Christopher Somerville meets with a man who has fulfilled the dream of so many people: to live self-sufficiently on a small island.

Unclouded Memories

Christopher Somerville

It took him ten years to find the right place, but when the advertisement appeared in *Exchange & Mart* magazine – 'Island More: house, boat, acre of garden, shellfish income' – Didi knew he could leave Germany behind for good. He bought the island house from the Englishman who had renovated it, moved in and began a life of fishing and organic gardening. The other Clew Bay islanders came over to Island More for a cup of tea, sniffed him over and decided he would do. There he was, occupant of a few hundred acres of grass and heather five miles out from Westport quay, with oyster beds to dredge and a run-down garden to work back into shape, a modest market for his shellfish and vegetables on his doorstep, a good roof over his head and a sheltering hill at his back. And there he remains, self-sufficient and self-contained, sharing the hard work and the unbroken peace of the island with Anne, fully intending to make old bones on Island More. On his trips into Westport he dives enthusiastically into local life, the pub gossip, the music and the crack. I heard plenty of grumbling against German 'blow-ins' buying up tracts of land in the west of Ireland, fencing off their property and making no effort to communicate with local people or to understand their way of life. But everyone in Westport had a good word for Didi.

The car in which Didi and Anne drove me to Rosmoney quay was an MOT inspector's nightmare, but it went. From the jetty we rowed out to a tiny fishing boat and puttered off through the maze of waterways between Clew Bay's islands. Croagh Patrick stood tall and dark over the bay, dominating the green-backed drumlins scattered at its feet, its conical head brushing the clouds. 'That's Inishlyre,' Didi said as we passed a low-lying island with a couple of houses tucked down on a pebbly bay. 'There's three families in it, fishing and farming. The old man still works as a pilot – Clew Bay has some bad waters.'

We anchored off Island More's stony strand, and splashed from the rowing boat up the beach and through the garden gate. If there is a more productive garden in the west of Ireland, I'd like to see it. The patient spade-work of Didi and Anne had filled the acre of ground between the wind-break hedges with a well-controlled riot of vegetables and fruit – lettuce, cabbage, broccoli and cauliflowers; asparagus and artichokes; parsnips, swedes and beetroot; shallots, onions and garlic; a mass of herbs; apples, plums, beans, sprouts. In the conservatory at the side of the house tomatoes hung in a jungle of leaves, and dried field mushrooms were threaded on strings among the rafters. 'This garden has never seen a drop of artificial fertiliser,' said Didi with quiet pride. 'We sell mainly to the sailing school on Collan More island just across the water there, and a little to the quality restaurants ashore. We make enough to keep going, as well as the fishing, you know.'

I had brought a bottle of Jameson's Irish whiskey and a hunk of goat cheese along with me, and there was no nonsense about saving the present till the guest had departed. Well warmed, Didi and I set off on a leisurely ramble around his little kingdom. Upwards of a hundred people had lived on Island More in the last century, raising cattle and crops, fishing the bay and the inshore waters. By 1950 they were all gone to softer beds and easier livelihoods on the mainland, though a few of the last inhabitants still retain ownership of small portions of the island and keep a couple of houses in good repair for the occasional visit. We scrambled over the grassy humps of old field boundaries, strolled the sloping meadows over orchids, birds'-foot trefoil and clover, stood for many minutes on the western cliffs looking out into the sunset over the crouching back of Clare Island ten miles offshore. A little window of prismatic colour, like a chip of rainbow, hung against the clouds over the Atlantic. The shingle spits of the Clew Bay islets shone like silver in the fading light, patterned on the water of the bay in a subtle and beautiful geometry. Down in the deserted village on the shore the island cows sheltered in the

ruined rooms where many of their now land-bound owners were conceived, born and reared. Didi kicked the thick carpet of dung in one of
the houses and grinned: 'This is where I get my fertiliser.'

Across the narrow waist of the island an abandoned pier drooped its
disintegrating stone finger into the bay, and here Didi settled himself on
a stone to roll a cigarette while I sat and gazed my fill at water, islet and
mountains. Walking back along the shore to the house in companionable
silence, Didi stopped and held up a warning hand. I peered ahead through
the half-light and saw what I had long dreamed of seeing – a big sea otter,
bounding across the stones ten yards away, his dark body undulating. He
slipped into the water with hardly a ripple and vanished. 'Gone fishing,'
said Didi.

How can one capture in words what can't be caught or pinned down
to time and place, even to a time and place as serene as Island More on
this still, sunlit evening? Among a lifetime's walks only a handful lie
unclouded in the memory, to be drawn out at will as if from a library and
walked and savoured again in their entirety. Island More is one of these.

Isle Of Man

John Betjeman writes of his visit to this island in the early 1950s when it was the holiday destination of hundreds of thousands of people from the north of England. Despite this extraordinary influx of tourists, Betjeman still finds places of peace and solitude where there are 'salt spray, seagulls, wild rocks and cavernous cliffs'.

An Isle Of Contrasts

John Betjeman

This brings me to the most enjoyable thing in all the enjoyment of Man – the visitors. I wish I knew when it was that these mass migrations from Lancashire started. Perhaps I can tell most easily from looking at Douglas. If I stand on Douglas Head and look across that noble sweep to Onchan Head, before the fairy lights are on and while the sun setting behind the mountains still lets me see the outline of the houses on the front, I can trace the recent history of the island.

The original Douglas at my feet, around the harbour, is a small fishing port, not half so beautiful as Castletown further down this eastern coast – Castletown with its magnificent medieval-moated and turreted castle, its box-pewed, three-deckered, still unspoilt church, its exciting stone police station by Baillie Scott, and its Doric column to Governor Smelt. What made Douglas grow was its natural scenery, but people did not notice natural scenery until Georgian times. The last Duke of Atholl to be governor had the Shrewsbury architect George Stewart design him, in 1804, a palace on this noble sweep of bay. It is known today in its smooth, silvery stone as Castle Mona Hotel. Its dining-room is the finest room on the island, the Adam style at its simplest and most graceful. Only that exquisite country house the Nunnery, in Walter Scott Gothic by John Pinch, compares with it. And after the Duke, the debtors escaping to Mona with some cash, and other visitors, built themselves romantic castles on these heights above the bay – Falcon Cliff, Fort Anne, Derby

Castle. These are late Georgian castellated buildings designed to look like romantic ruins by John Welch who also built in 1832 the Tower of Refuge on a rock in the middle of the water in Douglas Bay and so turned a looming danger into the semblance of an ancient castle. Then in the reign of William IV the gaps between the castles were filled in with stately stucco terraces, Brighton fashion (Windsor Terrace and Mount Pleasant are the best) sometimes high on the cliffs and here and there on the sea shore. The effect was and is magically beautiful. These Georgian terraces and Walter Scott, Peveril-of-the-Peak style castles flash out upon the cliff side. But this exclusive and romantic watering place cannot originally have been designed for half a million north-country folk – more likely for a few hundred half-pay officers eking out their pensions here where taxes are low.

I think the man of genius who turned the island into what it is, and saved it from ruin so that it is now financially prosperous, was Governor Loch. He improved the harbours and built the Loch Promenade in the sixties and seventies. Thereafter Douglas-style boarding-houses appeared in rows wherever there were gaps between the old terraces. They are innocent enough five-storeyed, bay-windowed, gabled buildings, gloomy behind, sea-gazing in front, rows and rows and rows of them so that the distant effect is of white paper folded into a concertina and perched here and there and everywhere along the shore. They are not as disfiguring as the modern bungalows and clumsily arranged electric light poles which ruin so much of the country part of Man. And now what with the TT, the motor races, the improved harbours, the way everybody is out to be gay, *however* gloomy you are feeling you cannot be ill-humoured in Douglas. The boats arrive, the aeroplanes come down, young men and old in open shirts, sports coats and grey flannels, young girls and old in cheerful summer dresses, queue for ices, queue for shrimps, crowd round bars for glasses of delicious dry champagne, gaze from horse-trams over municipal flowerbeds to the Tower of Refuge and the sea, travel in luxury coaches round the island half asleep in one another's arms till the sun sets behind the boarding-houses of Douglas and all the lights go up and the dance halls begin to fill. It is nine o'clock. There is still light in the sky. Father and mother, basking in one another's love, are sitting in chairs on the steps of the boarding-house; behind the front door peeps the inevitable castor oil plant in its china pot. Beside them sit the younger children, unnaturally good and quiet for fear they shall be sent up to bed while it is still light and while the moon rises huge and yellow above the purple bay. The elder children, grown up now, are off to the dance halls. Only a few rejected young men sit sadly on the steps among the ancients and the infants. The girls wear white dancing shoes and that is how you know whither they are bound. Two shillings or four-and-six, somewhere round that, is the cost of a ticket to dance. I like the Palace dance hall best. It has a parquet floor of sixteen thousand square feet and room for five thousand people. It is in a gay baroque style, cream and pink inside, and from the graceful roof hang Japanese lanterns out of a dangling forest of flags. A small and perfect dance band strikes up – ah, the dance bands of the Isle of Man! Soon a thousand couples are moving beautifully, the cotton dresses of the girls like vivid tulips in all this pale cream and pink, the sports coats and dark suits of the men a background to so much airy colour. The rhythmic dance is almost tribal, so that even a middle-aged spectator like me is caught up in mass excitement, pure and thrilling and profound.

And while the dance bands are playing in Douglas and the yellow moon is rising in its bay, on the western, wilder coast the herring fleet is setting out from Peel. The sun sets behind the rugged outline of the Castle and the ruined Cathedral and Round Tower enclosed within its walls. A stiffish west wind is blowing and the sea beyond the breakwater is dark green and choppy. The herring boats are disappearing into the sunset. Out of the harbour, round the castle island, the dying sun shines gold upon their polished sides. I stand alone upon a rock by Peel Castle. The smell of salt and wet earth is in my nostrils, the dark green slate of those old castle walls is at my side. Inland, the last rays of sun are lighting the winding lanes of Peel, the red sandstone of its church towers, and the soft protecting mountains behind it of the Isle of Man. Here, salt spray, seagulls, wild rocks and cavernous cliffs. Beyond those mountains the dance halls of Douglas and the dance-band leader in his faultless tails. An isle of contrasts! A miniature of all the Western world.

Gigha

Catherine Czerkawska writes of 'the largest community buyout in British history' when some six centuries of feudal control was overturned and a spirit of renewed hope was born among 'God's Islanders'.

Faith, Hope And Charity

Catherine Czerkawska

Looking at the history of Gigha, for so long held strange hostage to the fortunes and dispositions of successive owners, one is tempted to reiterate the old Scots saying that you can 'tell what the Good Lord thinks of money by the folks he gives it to.' With a few notable exceptions, Gigha has had its fair share of less than satisfactory landowners, from the days of the feuding McNeills and Allan nan Sop to more recent times. There can be few experiences more distressing than coming home to find an eviction notice chalked onto the door of your house because the landowner of the day has neglected to pay his debts.

The story of what was the largest community buyout in British history came about because Derek Holt, of Holt Leisure, who had owned the island for eleven years, decided that the time had come for him to leave Gigha and put the place on the market in August 2001. The real beginning of the buyout, however, probably came much earlier than that, with the accession of a Scottish parliament in 1999, and a corresponding sea change in the political will. The status quo was no longer seen to be satisfactory. Small communities, which until this time had been the passive recipients of the goodwill or otherwise of successive landowners, suddenly began to perceive that they might – with a certain amount of outside help and expertise – take control of their own destinies. Other communities, notably the Isle of Eigg, were already succeeding. The political will to support such buyouts was there, not least because the idea of a land reform bill, one which would give crofters the absolute right to compulsorily purchase the land upon which they lived and worked, was already in the offing, and would become law in 2003.

By the turn of the new millennium, with all its accompanying sense of new beginnings, the island had been under feudal control for some 600 years, so any change was always going to be of monumental proportions. The whole place, with the exception of a few council-owned homes and one or two private houses, was part of the 'estate' and was let out to tenants. When the island was advertised for sale for the last time, there were, apart from Achamore House, the hotel and six holiday cottages, thirty estate cottages, the post office, five let/partnership farms and two registered crofts. Some of these were 'retirement tenancies', many were 'short' (i.e. with security of tenure limited only to a period specified in the agreement), some were 'assured' and some few were 'protected'.

This in turn gave the landowner a large amount of freedom as to how he organised these various tenancies, how much he spent on maintenance of housing stock and how much leeway each individual tenant had to develop his or her property. In any case, there was little incentive for tenants to improve their houses for themselves, since many of them could be moved around the island on the whim of the landowner. It was this state of affairs that – with the accession of the new Scottish parliament – began to seem less and less tolerable to modern sensibilities.

There was much debate in the community, and a great deal of support by local MSP George Lyon. Willie McSporran, an islander born and bred, charismatic, occasionally brusque but widely respected and authoritative, was vocal in supporting the community buyout. When the islanders first met to discuss the possibility, there were only fourteen people in favour, but that was soon to change. Willie saw it not just as an opportunity but perhaps also as a last chance, while the island was still viable in terms of population numbers. But interest, casual or otherwise, was being shown in the island by the usual celebrity dreamers and investors, so time was of the essence. There was a referendum and some dissenting voices, but the upshot was that the islanders agreed to launch a bid to buy the island for themselves, and a steering committee of seven trusted members of the community was set up with Willie McSporran as chairman. This was the foundation of the Isle of Gigha Heritage Trust.

In 2002, Derek Holt sold the island to his tenants, in spite, so it was reported in the press, of a higher bid from some unknown source, for just over £4 million. The Scottish Land Fund (formed with £10 million from the New Opportunities Fund, part of the National Lottery) had offered the Trust £3.525 million, which with a grant of £500,000 from Highlands and Islands Enterprise, was enough to allow the community buyout to go ahead, on condition that £1 million of the money from the Scottish Land Fund would be treated as a loan and would be paid back by March 2004, in just two years' time. The Trust was confident that the sale of Achamore House (although not the gardens, which were reserved to the Trust) as well as some other small pieces of land, would account for a large percentage of the sum, but it left some £200,000, which would have to be raised by a hundred islanders. It must have seemed a tall order, but there is a diaspora of those for whom Gigha was once home, as well as all those people who had visited and fallen in love with the place over the years.

On 15 March 2002, in a ceremony that was televised all over Britain to the accompaniment of media emotions that ranged from unbounded joy, through caution to downright criticism, the island was handed over to the Trust. Stone and earth of the land of Gigha, the traditional symbols of a change of ownership, were given over to Willie McSporran, representing the people of the island. The 'New Dawn' had come for Gigha. A nominated director from Highlands and Islands Enterprise joined the seven directors of the Trust. One of their first tasks, quite apart from the momentous undertaking of repaying the debt, was to ensure a smooth transition for the hotel and its accompanying holiday cottages, which were booked up well in advance. Improvements would have to be made, but initially at any rate, it must have been a case of making assessments and making sure that nothing went too disastrously wrong in the transitional period. Those who expected a sudden and complete change overnight would be doomed to disappointment. Nothing so momentous is ever quite so easy. But once the islanders had bought their island, a powerful will to make things work was born.

Islay

James Hunter relates how two tiny islands on an island loch was once the principal residence of the Lords of the Isles who, with their dynasties of artists, musicians and sculptors, ruled over a large part of Scotland for over a century.

Lords Of The Isles

James Hunter

Although I live in Skye, of all the Hebrides Islay has long been the island I like best. Its people – those whom I know anyway – seem to me to give the place a friendly feel. And it so happens that my visits have practically always coincided with spells of good weather; weather of the kind which produces sunlight strong enough to show the full range of colour contrasts you get around the likes of Loch Indaal. Bright blue waters; bright green fields; clusters of white-painted buildings perched here and there between the two: these are the impressions of Islay which linger in my mind.

This evening, towards the end of August, Islay is not at all like that. The day has been one of the sort which in the west of Ireland they call *tais*, or soft. It is not wet exactly; not even drizzling. But the wind off the Atlantic is so moist as to make the air feel definitely damp. The atmosphere, as a result, has taken on a peculiarly milky quality. The landscape has something of the appearance of slightly faded watercolour. The horizon has no hard edge to it. And when I look out from Bowmore, in the direction of Port Charlotte and Bruichladdich, the rising ground behind these communities seems simply to merge with the steadily lowering clouds.

The road northwards from Bowmore begins by skirting the extensive mudflats at the head of Loch Indaal. Then, just before Bridgend, it plunges suddenly into the heavily wooded policies surrounding Islay House. Here I turn into the shallow valley of the River Sorn, passing a succession of productive-looking farms of the type which, despite the agricultural industry's many recent difficulties, are still common enough hereabouts.

Its underlying Hebridean character is so evident as to make it wrong to say that Islay's farms give its landscape a wholly Lowland look. But they certainly differentiate the place markedly from the predominantly crofting islands further north; as do Islay's several villages which – for all that none of them, not even Bowmore, are very large by mainland standards – are older and more concentrated settlements than those you typically find in the Highland part of Scotland.

A mile or so beyond one such village, Ballygrant, I pause at a junction and take the narrow road to my left. The road soon becomes a track. Once it led to Finlaggan Farm, but the farm has for some time been abandoned. Loose sheets of rusting corrugated iron lie about its overgrown yard. The roofs of its once substantial steadings are collapsing gradually inwards; their rafters projecting from among their thinning slates in much the same way as the ribs of those long dead sheep – which you come across occasionally while walking among the Highland hills – can be seen jutting through the gaps in their tightly stretched and slowly rotting sides.

Agriculture has been recently replaced by forestry in much of this north-eastern corner of Islay, and forestry does not keep people on the land. This is an emptied countryside. Far too many of its cottages and farmhouses have that strangely hollow look you get about a former dwelling when its window-panes and window-frames have gone. Hillsides which once supported sheep and cattle have been given over now to conifers.

Leaving my car at the track's end, I follow the path leading towards Loch Finlaggan. There is more dereliction here. On two small islands, not far from the loch's eastern extremity, are the crumbling remnants of a number of buildings. Standing out darkly against the cloudy western sky and the rough waters of the loch, these ruins, while stark enough, do not seem terribly impressive. They have nothing of the grandeur of Edinburgh Castle. And their surroundings – which consist mostly of gently rounded hills – make this a scenically less spectacular place than, for example, Iona.

'But there was a time when Finlaggan was as important as anywhere in Scotland,' I had been told a little earlier by an Islay farmer, Donald Bell. So it was. For Finlaggan, in the fourteenth and fifteenth centuries, was the main centre of the Lordship of the Isles. And it was this semi-independent principality which, for more than a hundred years, went no small way to providing Gaelic-speaking Scots with an organisational focus of the kind which had been lost as a result of the anglicisation of the Scottish monarchy.

Here at Finlaggan, on the larger of these two islands, Eilean Mor, successive Lords of the Isles maintained their most important residence. On the smaller island, Eilean na Comhairle, there met the lordship's governing council. Here, too, as was long afterwards recalled by Hugh MacDonald, a seventeenth century historian and tradition-bearer from Skye, the Lords of the Isles were formally installed in office – their installation, as described by the Skye *seannachie*, being very reminiscent of the coronation ceremonies once conducted in Dalriada.

A bishop was always present at the inauguration of a Lord of the Isles, MacDonald observed. And the bishop was accompanied, it seemed, by 'seven priests' as well as by 'the chieftains of all the principal families' then occupying the lordship's extensive territories.

At Finlaggan, MacDonald continued, 'there was a square stone, seven or eight feet long, and the tract of a man's foot cut thereon'. Each new Lord of the Isles stood on this carved stone, 'denoting that he should walk in the footsteps of his predecessors'. And it was in this upright position, MacDonald explained, that the lordship's leaders entered into their inheritance.

The Finlaggan stone – which evidently possessed the same sort of spiritual significance as both the Scottish Stone of Destiny and the Irish Stone of Kings on which the O'Neill chieftains of Tyrone were traditionally inaugurated prior to its being smashed to pieces by the English in 1601 – has long since disappeared. It is hard now, on these deserted islands where the summer's growth of waist-high vegetation makes it difficult to discern even the foundations of most of the many buildings which once stood here, to recapture the tremendous sense of occasion which must have surrounded the installing of a Lord of the Isles.

'He was clothed in a white habit to show his innocence and integrity of heart,' said Hugh MacDonald of one of the men whose rule began here in Finlaggan. 'He received a white rod in his hand, intimating that he had the power to govern, not with tyranny and partiality but with discretion and sincerity.' A sword was then handed over, MacDonald continued, in order to signify the means by which the people of the lordship expected their leader 'to protect and defend them from the incursions of their enemies'. These ceremonies being concluded, 'mass was said ... the people pouring out their prayers for the success and prosperity of their new-created lord.'

Jane Dawson writes movingly of her husband who in death becomes one with the island he grew to love.

Circle of Heather

Jane Dawson

Rod's coffin was brought back to Islay on the early morning ferry next day so at about the time the hearse would be passing on its way to Portnahaven Church, I climbed to the top of Corner Hill. It was a fantastic view and from my high seat I could see the site of the grave on top of the Beinn in one direction and the roof of our house at the other; where I was sitting was at a point on a straight line between the grave and the house. I had a very strong feeling that Rod was not in the coffin at all; he was in the heather, the wild flowers, the grasses, the butterflies and even the air around me; there was nothing in the coffin but an empty body.

As the hearse went past on the road below I noticed a Hen Harrier flying alongside it for nearly 100 yards. I heard later that as the coffin was being lifted from the hearse, a Merlin swooped down and the coffin bearers had to duck to avoid it.

The funeral took place next day and Portnahaven Church was absolutely crammed. It was agreed that no women should follow the coffin to the grave, so the remaining mourners who accompanied the specially made wooden bier each took their turn at carrying Rod's body to its final resting place. As the procession wound its way up the steep slopes of the Beinn, I learned later that a Golden Eagle was seen soaring overhead.

That evening Dine and Rod's mother accompanied me up to the grave, thankful for the lift on a tractor trailer for a large part of the way. From the top of the Beinn we could see Colonsay to the north with the mountains of Mull behind it, Jura to the east, Rathlin Island and Ireland to the south.

Below us stretched the lands of Ellister which had given Rod so much pleasure. The grave itself was covered with the flowers brought up on the bier and at the head of the grave was Dine's wreath of heather.

The children and I climbed up to Rod's grave every 13th August, whatever the weather, and were thrilled to see a circle of heather growing where the wreath had taken root. There are only rushes and grasses in the surrounding area.

Jura

In this letter to the author, George Woodcock, George Orwell relates how he assisted his neighbour in the harvest of his crops in the traditional manner of generations of Hebridean crofters who undertook the vital tasks communally. He revealingly notes how the crofters are in many respects 'better off and more independent than a town labourer'.

Letters From Barnhill

George Orwell

Barnhill, 2 September 1946

Dear George,

Thanks ever so for the tea – it came just at the right moment because this week the whole of the nearest village is being brought here in lorries to get in the field of corn in front of our house, and of course tea will have to flow like water while the job is on. We have been helping the crofter who is our only neighbour with his hay and corn, at least when rain hasn't made it impossible to work. Everything is done here in an incredibly primitive way. Even when the field is ploughed with a tractor the corn is still sown broadcast, then scythed and bound up into sheaves by hand. They seem to broadcast corn, i.e. oats, all over Scotland, and I must say they seem to get it almost as even as can be done by a machine. Owing to the wet they don't get the hay in till about the end of September or even later, sometimes as late as November, and they can't leave it in the open but have to store it all in lofts. A lot of the corn doesn't quite ripen and is fed to the cattle in sheaves like hay. The crofters have to work very hard, but in many ways they are better off and more independent than a town labourer, and they would be quite comfortable if they could get a bit of help in the way of machinery, electrical power and roads, and could get the landlords off their backs and get rid of the deer. These animals are so common on this particular island that they are an absolute curse. They eat up the pastures where there ought to be sheep, and they make fencing immensely more expensive than it need be. The crofters aren't allowed to shoot them, and are constantly having to waste their time dragging carcases of deer down from the hill during the stalking season. Everything is sacrificed to the brutes because they are an easy source of meat and therefore profitable to the people who own them. I suppose sooner or later these islands will be taken in hand, and then they could either be turned into a first-rate area for dairy produce and meat, or else they would support a large population of small peasants living off cattle and fishing. In the 18th century the population here was 10,000 – now less than 300.

My love to Inge. I hope to be back in London about October 13th.

Yours
George

In this letter to Sonia Brownell, who was to become his second wife some two years later, Orwell relates the complex travel arrangements required to reach Jura which sound rather like a military campaign.

Barnhill, 12 April 1947

Dearest Sonia,

I am handwriting this because my typewriter is downstairs. We arrived OK & without incident yesterday. Richard was as good as gold & rather enjoyed having a sleeper to himself after he had got over the first strangeness, & as soon as we got into the plane at Glasgow he went to sleep, probably because of the noise. I hadn't been by plane before & I think it's really better. It costs £2 or £3 more, but it saves about 5 hours & the boredom of going on boats, & even if one was sick it's only three quarters of an hour whereas if one goes by sea one is sick for five or six hours, i.e. if it is bad weather. Everything up here is just as backward as in England, hardly a bud showing & I saw quite a lot of snow yesterday. However it's beautiful spring weather now & the plants I put in at the new year seem to be mostly alive. There are daffodils all over the place, the only flower out. I'm still wrestling with more or less virgin meadow, but I think by next year I'll have quite a nice garden here. Of course we've had a nightmare all today getting things straight, with Richard only too ready to help, but it's more or less right now & the house is beginning to look quite civilised. It will be some weeks before we've got the transport problem fully solved, but otherwise we are fairly well appointed. I'm going to send for some hens as soon as we have put the hen house up, & this year I have been also able to arrange for alcohol so that one has just a little, a sort of rum ration, each day. Last year we had to be practically TT. I think in a week everything will be straight & the essential work in the garden done, & then I can get down to some work.

I wrote to Janetta asking her to come whenever she liked & giving instructions about the journey. So long as she's bringing the child, not just sending it, it should be simple enough. I want to give you the complete details about the journey, which isn't so formidable as it looks on paper. The facts are these:

There are boats to Jura on Mondays, Wednesdays & Fridays. You have to catch the boat train at Glasgow at 8 am, which means that it's safer to sleep the preceding night at Glasgow, because the all-night trains have a nasty way of coming in an hour or two hours late, & then one misses the boat train. The times & so on are as follows:

8 am leave Glasgow Central for GOUROCK.
Join boat for Tarbert (TARBET) at Gourock.
Abt 12 noon arrive East Tarbert.
Travel by bus to West Tarbert (bus runs in conjunction with the boats).
Join boat for CRAIGHOUSE (Jura) at West Tarbert.
Abt 3.30 pm arrive Craighouse.
Take hired car to LEALT, where we meet you.
If you want to go by plane, the planes run daily (except Sundays I think),

& they nearly always take off unless it's very misty.

The itinerary then is:

10.30 arrive at Scottish Airways office at St Enoch Station, Glasgow (the air office is in the railway station).

10.40 leave by bus for RENFREW.

11.15 leave by plane for ISLAY. (Pronounced EYELY).

12 noon arrive Islay.

Hire a car (or take bus) to the ferry which leads to Jura.

Abt 1 pm cross ferry.

Hired car to LEALT.

It's important to let us know in advance when you are coming, because of the hired car. There are only 2 posts a week here, & only 2 occasions on which I can send down to Craighouse to order the car. If you come by boat, you could probably get a car all right by asking on the quay, but if you come by air there wouldn't be a car at the ferry (which is several miles from Craighouse) unless ordered beforehand. Therefore if you proposed coming on, say, June 15th, it wld be as well to write abt June 5th because, according to the day of the week, it may be 4 or 5 days before your letter reaches me, & another 3 or 4 days before I can send a message. It's no use wiring because the telegrams come by the postman.

You want a raincoat & if possible stout boots or shoes – gum boots if you have them. We may have some spare gum boots, I'm not sure. We are fairly well off for spare oilskins & things like that. It wld help if you brought that week's rations, because they're not quick at getting any new-comer's rations here, & a little flour & tea.

I am afraid I am making this all sound very intimidating, but really it's easy enough & the house is quite comfortable. The room you wld have is rather small, but it looks out on the sea. I do so want to have you here. By that time I hope we'll have got hold of an engine for the boat, & if we get decent weather we can go round to the completely uninhabited bays on the west side of the island, where there is beautiful white sand & clear water with seals swimming abt in it. At one of them there is a cave where one can take shelter when it rains, & at another there is a shepherd's hut which is disused but quite livable where one could even picnic for a day or two. Anyway do come, & come whenever you like for as long as you like, only try to let me know beforehand. And meanwhile take care of yourself & be happy.

I've just remembered I never paid you for that brandy you got for me, so enclose £3. I think it was abt that wasn't it? The brandy was very nice & was much appreciated on the journey up because they can't get alcohol here at all easily. The next island, Islay, distils whisky, but it all goes to America. I gave the lorry driver a large wallop, more than a double, & it disappeared so promptly that it seemed to hit the bottom of his belly with a click.

With much love

George

Roger Deakin explores the island on which George Orwell created the malevolent, all-seeing Big Brother within sight of the Paps – breasts – which early settlers worshipped as symbols of a maternal deity who benignly watched over their every move.

Orwell's Whirlpool
Roger Deakin

Poring over the map of Jura in the library back in Cambridge, with its bewildering choice of swimmable water, I had nearly resorted to planning my journey by throwing darts blindfold at the map. To know the island as I do is only to realise how much more there will always be to discover of its beauties and difficulties. It resists you at every step. For a swimmer, it combines heaven and hell. It has delicious water and dramatic beaches, but also a menacing whirlpool and some of the fiercest tidal currents in the British Isles. There is only one road, almost no footpaths (just deer-tracks), it rains a good deal, and in summer there are midges. It is really a tawny desert, with less than 250 people on 160 square miles of island. This is why you can wander on the face of Jura for days without meeting a living soul, and it is probably why George Orwell came to live here in April 1946.

Orwell had first visited Jura in September 1945, at the suggestion of his friend David Astor, whose family owned an estate on the island. It hadn't occurred to anyone that the trip was more than a holiday, but when the writer heard that a remote farmhouse near the north coast was available, he decided to move in. His wife, Eileen, died suddenly that winter, and he temporarily abandoned the plan, but by April 1946 he was moving into Barnhill. The house was twenty-five miles from the nearest shop. It had no electricity and no telephone, and only the roughest of tracks leading up to it for the last five miles, but Orwell was anxious to get out of London, and wanted his three-year-old son Richard to grow up in the country. What could be better for a small boy than a wild island? He set about farming and gardening in a small way, went fishing, planted fruit trees. Bought one rowing boat with an outboard engine, and began writing *Nineteen Eighty Four*. The hardship and the adventure of the place must have appealed to him. But as desert places, the Western Isles were also where the Celtic saints retreated to hear the voice of God in the silence. Orwell, writing his prophetic novel about politics and the human soul, needed somewhere silent to hear himself think his own special brand of common sense

It was late afternoon by the time I arrived on the remote white sand beach of Glenbatrick Bay on the far west coast of Jura. On the neighbouring island of Islay I had enquired amongst the fishermen on the quayside for a boatman and was told, 'If it's Glenbatrick you want, that's your man.' They pointed out a commanding figure loading up a sleek rubber-hulled powerboat who turned out to be the laird himself, Lord Astor, fetching provisions for his solitary island cottage. He readily agreed to take me over the Sound of Islay with him.

I dived into the loch in the calm, clear sand-warmed water of Glenbatrick Bay. It is a wild, enchanted shore fortified by a succession of steep rocky ridges running out from the high ground like break waters to the sea, each sheltering a sand or a pebble beach. I swam on the rising tide, keeping an eye on my rucksack, like a milestone on the beach as I drifted perceptibly up the loch. Two seals watched me idly from one of the rocks that stand out everywhere like crocodiles' teeth until the tide conceals them. There were otters here too. The dazzling sun burnt a furrow straight down the loch, and shone on the heathery pelt of the island, which looked easy walking from out in the sea, although I knew it wasn't. I turned and struck back towards the beach, with the white stone cottage at its edge, and a backdrop of the three rounded summits of the Paps, curiously striped with streaks of white quartzite as though gigantic prehistoric birds have roosted and shat on them for millions of years. The tallest of them always seems to have a white cloud hovering just above it, like Kilimanjaro.

Julie Brook spends summers living in one of Jura's numerous caves and creates works of art out of driftwood.

Cave Artist
Alistair Scott

She was thirty-one and had been born into the Navy which, she said, meant she came from nowhere in particular. England had been her home but now it was Scotland. Glasgow and a Jura cave. At first she had been afraid of the nights, the sounds and the occasional stranger who stumbled on her home. But now she was used to it, the noises, smells, sights; it felt like home. She was five months into her second summer here. Like Gavin Maxwell in *Ring of Bright Water,* she found the sea provided all her needs in driftwood form.

Around us, on easels and stacked against the wall, were her canvases of mountain scenery; bold impressionist splashes in oil covering sixteen, twenty-four square feet at a time. Most were streaked with rain. A life spent without hangovers among tall walls was, I felt, the criterion for peaceful co-existence with Julie's exuberant work. Her wood rubbings I really liked. She had taken them from the broken ribs of a boat, and into each she had incised a question or phrase in exquisite italics: *how old is the tree? . . . what seas has the ship sailed? . . . the storms that broke them . . . green light in the copper nail . . .*

'I had an exhibition in Craighouse recently as a sort of thank you to the people who've been so kind. Just to show them the sort of things I'm doing here. Most didn't like my work but at least they felt sufficiently comfortable to say so.' But enough people in the rest of the country did like her work. Her largest pictures fetched over £2,000. She made me feel words were a mug's game.

'What I love here is how the seed of an idea grows. It grows in a way you can never predict and out of it comes all sorts of other seeds. That's how I got into fire stacks'

I still didn't understand fire stacks if they weren't for good old-fashioned pillage, but it was time to go and Julie was explaining my role. She had made a raft from wood and flotsam and odds and ends. She would paddle out to the stack, load it with wood, throw on turps and ignite it. I was to hold the raft's rope, counteract the westerly Gulf Stream, and haul her in when she gave the word. I had horrible premonitions about all this. I could see another Julie in years to come with a fragment of this Julie's raft, carving: *. . . what seas has she sailed? . . .*

'OK?' she asked.

'Go easy with the turps.'

We trooped out on our secret mission. It was still too secret for my liking. 'What are these fire stacks all about?'

'I want to create fire on the surface of the sea, to explore their relationship.'

Fire. Sea. Relationship. I thought I understood. She was surely looking for what the *National Geographic* Picture Desk calls 'moments'. ('We need *moments*, you understand? Gesture, action, emotion but real moments, as they happen . . .') They were Gasp or Nod Factors. Then I knew I didn't understand. I couldn't see the point of building cairns for the sea to knock down and bonfires for waves to extinguish.

'The point is that if something has no function it can be appreciated solely for what it is. For example, a kiln is a brilliant creation. The fire is often more beautiful than the pottery it produces, but it's neglected and regarded only for its function. The fire stack has no function. We can therefore see it with uncluttered vision for its true worth.' She climbed onto the raft. 'You got the other end of the rope? OK, give me a shove.'

She paddled out towards America. The wind was rising. Five minutes later flames leapt up from the fire stack.

'PULL.'

I pulled, thinking how absurd it all was, one of my more bizarre experiences, hauling on a rope in the dark, pulling in a woman who was no more than a bobbing headlight on a homemade raft adrift in a choppy Atlantic with a piece of fish box for a paddle.

Smudges of cloud crept along the horizon's glow, – a lurid red except where Colonsay's blackness lay stretched out like a resting lizard. Julie walked out of the ocean, rummaged in a bag, produced a couple of stemmed glasses and poured liberal measures of Isle of Jura 10-Year-Old Single Malt. We drank to fire stacks and looked out to sea.

'Brilliant!'

I saw a bonfire on a pile of stones. I think Julie saw creation. But it was, without question, a moment.

Iona

One of the finest Hebridean poets of the 20th century, Iain Crichton Smith visits this cradle of Christianity. Although a life-long atheist, Smith is nonetheless deeply impressed by the Iona Community who seek to act according to the vision of the early Celtic Church and by its founder, Lord MacLeod who, like himself, 'kept the human and the poetic at the centre of his consciousness'.

How Vulnerable We Are

Iain Crichton Smith

The last time I was on Iona was in the summer of 1955. It was a blazing blue day, and it seemed as near to Heaven as one could get. I remember from that visit wandering about the graveyard and noticing with a certain pathos the headstone of a nameless sailor whose body had been washed up on the shore in 1945.

This time the weather was a sinister battleship grey, and the neighbouring island, known as the Dutchman's Cap, resembled a submarine, with its conning tower highly visible above the water. On my arrival, I was drenched by a cold persistent perpendicular rain. The first old building I came to was the nunnery whose walls were being strengthened. The windows of the primary school look out onto this ruined 15th century building which has a little garden in its centre with poppies and wild geraniums growing in profusion. Rooks cawed round it, and there were seagulls. In the coffee house run by the Community I met a girl from Sussex who was serving there. She was doing voluntary work and was staying for six weeks at the MacLeod Centre. She had been before and enjoyed it. Later I met two Swedish ladies walking barefoot through the rain. It occurred to me that for Columba and his followers there must not only have been fine days but days like this as well, of weeping seeping rains, as they sailed about the islands. But on fine gem-like days, it must also have been close to Heaven.

The Abbey itself seemed simple and ornamental. In its living quarters, a large number of people sat, doing their chores, creating a brief community with each other, coming and going like the waves of the sea. Many had been before. At lunch I talked to a young Anglican doing Religious Studies at Bangor. We chatted about women priests. 'They will definitely come', he said optimistically.

In the bookshop there were books on ecology, on Celtic religious consciousness, on South African and South American politics. One that caught my eye was called *Christ in a Poncho*. Curiously, standing nearby was a Christ-like young man, who had a gingery beard and an ankle-length knitted woollen coat of many colours. Actually, he was a rarity: most of the others were conventionally dressed.

'What Lord MacLeod really wanted to do was start a brotherhood', the Reverend John Harvey, leader of the Iona Community, told me. 'His original intention was to have ministers come to the island, before they started work in their parishes, and labour alongside unemployed craftsmen. Now the emphasis has changed somewhat because there is not the rebuilding work to do'. I asked him about the place of women in the Community. 'Of course, there were no women ministers in the church when the work was started. Now the proportion is perhaps one third women to two thirds men'.

According to Warden Philip Newell, women were leaders in the Celtic Church. 'In the Celtic Church Mary is not seen as the High Queen of Heaven, but as the barefooted country girl'. How did he think this church would have developed as distinct from the Roman Catholic? 'The Celts had a sense of Heaven and Earth as being inescapably bonded together. The Earth was shot through with the presence of God. There was no spirit/matter divide.' In the tranquillity of Iona, I thought that they might very well have been justified in their thinking. After all, the Book of Kells, said to have been made here, is an inexhaustible radiant masterpiece.

*   *   *

Later, I went for a walk. The island was marvellously tranquil. Lambs separated from mothers by fences were bleating perplexedly. The sands were brilliantly white. Flowers grew everywhere. I met an islander who greeted me in Gaelic. It was strange to think of this 'laboratory' or hot-house set on an island. It reminded me of a Cairngorm brooch with a jewel at its centre. The eternal sea flounced against the rocks. There were cows and horses. I remembered Columba's horse which was supposed to have nuzzled him at the end. The air of Iona, according to Lord MacLeod, was very thin, not much separated Earth and Heaven.

Two things come to mind. I thought first of the unknown sailor gathered at the end into a community he had never known. But also of something else.... I was once travelling from Glasgow to Oban on the train. There were two other people in the carriage. One was shy, specta-cled, young. He was reading a book and I assumed for some reason that he was a student. The other was a blind-drunk Rangers supporter wear-ing the obligatory blue scarf and clutching the obligatory lager can. He ranted on about the 'F..... Fenians.' He talked about Rabbie Burns, and 'a man's a man for a' that' I found it hard to see the spiritual in the material but perhaps I should have tried.

I met the student later in the corridor. It turned out that he was German and that he was on his way to Iona, to stay with the Community. I told him not to mention that to our companion, whom he would have seen as some blue blazing monster.

I recall thinking at the time, what would have happened if a Celtic Church had taken over, gentle unbureaucratic, with a feminine as well as a masculine psyche, perhaps undogmatic and exploratory? An armour of hostile righteousness clothed my Rangers friend. How had this come to pass, how was someone so irreligious speaking in the name of religion? Most of all I despised myself for nodding and nodding, for violence was not far from the surface.

Lord MacLeod, autocratic, mystical, a living paradox of the aristocrat who heard the cries of the poor, did not nod and nod. He was a fighter. If I were a believer in God, I would have found him irresistible. He kept the human and the poetic at the centre of his consciousness. In a Scottish religious situation which has tended to focus on the intellectual, he insist-ed on the holistic. The rigid Calvinism which he reacted against is being, as far as I can see, washed over by the tides. It was his ability to see this that made him a great man and a great visionary. We have to learn to live non-violently together. We have to learn to walk naked without the armour of dogma.

It seemed appropriate that day that I saw a snail without its shell. The water trembled and winked. How vulnerable we are. The ferry set off. It was both necessary to come to Iona and to leave it. So must Celtic missionaries have felt in their explorations and returns, on the endlessly mobile sea which is itself a metaphor for life.

Inchkenneth

Neil MacGillvray worked as a boatman and gardener on this tiny island once owned by the extraordinary Mitford family. Here he talks about the tragic aftermath of Unity Mitford's passion for Adolph Hitler.

Hitler and Chocolate Éclairs

Neil MacGillvray

Unity was the strangest of them all. She was the fourth daughter and she was born in August 1914, the month the Great War broke out. Her first name, Unity, must have been a plea for peace, but her second name was Valkyrie, a very Wagnerian and very warlike name. She was a beautiful, Teutonic, Aryan-looking woman. She went off to Germany in the 'thirties and fell in love with Hitler and the Third Reich. She lived a hectic life in Munich, courting and being courted by the fashionable aristocratic elite. Her nickname was 'Bobo'. She and Eva Braun were Hitler's two favourites. Hitler tried to use her to build fences with Britain. I've read that the happiest moment of her life was 'sitting at the Fuhrer's feet while he stroked her hair'. She used to speak of how beautiful and blue his eyes were. How much he liked chocolate éclairs. She's supposed to have reported, 'He abstained from sex', but if Unity didn't have sex with Hitler she certainly enjoyed it with others. She had a racing MG open-top, and used to drive around in low-cut dresses, singing; flags and pennants streaming behind her on the Alpine roads. She had an affair with Count Almacy, the German spy on whom the novel and the film *The English Patient* is based. After bedtime prayers, it's said, she would give a Nazi salute before jumping into bed. Of course, that was long before she came here to Inchkenneth.

When I knew her she sometimes had difficulty walking. You see it came as a terrible shock for Unity when war was declared on 3rd September 1939. That same day she went out into the English garden in

Munich and shot herself in the head. The two nations she loved were at war. She left a note to the Fuhrer: 'Be merciful to my people'. She must have assumed Hitler all-powerful. The bullet lodged in her brain. She was rushed to hospital but the bullet was not retrievable. Very slowly she recuperated with the bullet still there in her head, until, on the Fuhrer's personal orders, she was evacuated through Switzerland back to Britain. Doctors said, at best, she would live ten years, and that's what she did.

Lady Redesdale wanted to bring her up to Inchkenneth to convalesce in tranquillity, but Koch na Leal, the sea loch in which Inchkenneth lies, was an important naval anchorage and the security people thought she might radio information to the enemy. So it was not until 1944, after the invasion of Europe, and shortly after her sister Diana was released from prison, that she was brought north. Although, once the war started, Mosley urged his Fascist followers to join up and fight against Hitler, he was not trusted and both he and Diana were imprisoned for four years. Still, once Unity arrived she spent the rest of her life on Inchkenneth. She would walk in the garden and sit for hours on the pier, wrapped in a blanket, looking out to sea. And she would come over to the post office at Gribun, and she would come over for dances at the school. That's when I would dance with her. The boatman on Inchkenneth then was Baldy MacFadyan, but sometimes, late at night, I would ferry her back to the island and we got on very well.

There's a very old chapel on the island and when visitors came they would sometimes hold services there. Later on I used to read the lesson myself. She was only thirty-four when she died. It was John MacFadyan who brought her back over the water for the last time and she was carried on a stretcher and put on the ferry at Craignure and taken up to the cottage hospital in Oban. The death certificate states that she died from an 'old gunshot wound'. Her death came within weeks of the ten years that the German doctors had originally diagnosed, and four years after Hitler shot himself in the bunker.

Many people will say she deserved all she got, and Hitler deserved much worse than he got. However, it's still a tragic story.

She had a small bedroom on the second floor of the house, but her bed was a grand four-poster with sagging green drapes, pale and worn thin with age. She was not a Fascist when I knew her. She and her mother used to entertain the local children at Gribun with parties at Eastertime, and I remember watching her in the kitchen, cracking eggs to make a cake. She had become very absent-minded and she just kept cracking eggs – three or four dozen she cracked into a great bowl and then whipped them up. I didn't say anything. I was not employed on the island at that time; I was just helping out with the boats, so I said nothing.

Eigg

The poet, Kathleen Raine, who had a long unrequited love for Gavin Maxwell, is compelled to ask many profound questions about the nature of place, culture and consciousness when she first sets foot on this Hebridean island.

Spiritual Geography

Kathleen Raine

Is there a spiritual geography, are there certain places upon the earth which are more, or less, attuned to certain modes of consciousness? And if so, do such qualities belong to the earth itself, to certain qualities of light, or sound, or scent, or rock formation? Is there a natural magic, and elemental spirits who inhabit certain places, or kinds of place? Or do people of a certain cast of mind impart to the land their own qualities? It seems not to be true, as Wordsworth sometimes seems to imply, that 'nature' can impart a culture; and the people of Cumberland and Northumberland (whatever they were in the Border Ballad days) are prosaic enough. Hardy's people had a sense of history, yet only Hardy has made poetry of their lives. But in the Highlands I found people who possessed a culture; a culture not only deeper than that of the Northumbrians of my childhood, but also than positivist Cambridge. Oral tradition still transmitted, not merely the history of the race and its memories, but certain ancient attitudes and values lost to the technological present. I was already at this time, though still blindly, seeking for the lost thread of another tradition altogether than the materialist civilization dominant in England; dominant no less in poetry and the arts (as I had discovered to my cost in Cambridge) than in science and technology. My friend Herbert Read continued to believe that its arts can save that civilization; but I had come to see in its arts only another symptom of the spiritual disease of which it is dying.

It was in the June, following my meeting with Gavin that Winifred

Nicholson and I went for the first time to Eigg; her to paint, me to write. 'You can see the flash of my lighthouse from the *sgurr,*' Gavin had said; and for me, Eigg was above all an isle from which I could see the flash of his light. But that is the character of the Isles where summit and skerry are seamarks known to every boatman and shepherd, and the unchanging scene into which life is woven through the generations, from isle to isle, and so is likely to be so long as the mountains of Rhum and Canna's Compass Hill stand against the winds and the seas. Indeed are not all Scots bound into nationhood by a landscape of isles and mountains known to all? And were we not all once so bound to the earth itself, for countless generations before we were driven into the exile of the modern urban scene, ever-shifting and impermanent, where all sense of continuity of the generations is lost? 'I don't know how humanity stands it,' as Ezra Pound said.

On midsummer eve, I remember, we climbed the hill for the first time to the point where the road looks down to Cleadale, the crofters' village facing to the west. The long evening light was magical; Winifred painted a picture of Rhum, which I was not able to see until the paint had dried and the multitudes of adhering midges could be brushed off. From below we heard two girls singing as they gathered up their washing from the machair. Those lovely voices heard in the absence of all mechanical noise, where only the cries of sheep and birds and the sound of the sea accompanied their singing is something not to be heard any more; for the television sets have reached the outermost isles, and the sounds there now are what they are elsewhere. I did not know then that I was hearing for almost the last time something so simple and so familiar to mankind from the beginning. But it was not so much the past that we seemed there to enter, but the permanent, the enduring norm, the familiar.

We had taken rooms in the somewhat bleak manse; but we were lent an empty house at Kildonan, site of an early monastic settlement. Each day, Winifred painted in one room, while I wrote in the other. Happy, productive days. But whereas for Winifred, whose roots are so deep in the past of Cumberland, it was an adventure into a beautiful strange land, for me it was like a recovery of a lost identity, a re-grafting to an old root, though already long severed when I was born. For our tea we boiled water drawn from the near-by spring on just such a kitchen range as I had known at Bavington. Of course I was not really returning home; it was only as if; yet Gavin's lighthouse flashing its message made it seem so.

On Eigg that summer, and later on the mainland and on other Isles, I came to know people whose simplicity of life was permeated with an essential quality of which poetry is the natural speech; Homer might have sung in those kitchens by turf fires, with shepherds' dogs under the table and the wooden chairs drawn back round the walls. On Eigg there was a bard – Hugh MacKinnon – who composed his verses stretched at length on the kitchen bench, a cap over his eyes; a tradition handed down from the Bardic schools where the *fili* composed their verses lying on their beds and in darkness. In such company I found myself not, as in England, too much a poet, but not poet enough, for I could neither sing nor recite, as all did here, their learning all stored in their memory. I had been away too long by several generations, although indeed in my grandmother's kitchen people had sung – all my mother's sisters had sweet voices and memories stored with the songs of the Lowlands. In the house of Hugh MacKinnon I heard stories of things done and suffered by men and women whose houses now were just green mounds. For the bard is the guardian of memories, and the maker of stories that still brought grief and joy and laughter to the descendants of those vanished ancestors. There were stories too, that included the inner, the supernatural event; I first met the 'Celtic twilight' not through books but at the source itself; a privilege the more treasured as it was unsought.

Eilean Shona

J.M. Barrie was invited to stay in this tiny island's mansion from time to time and in this letter to a literary friend, he conveys his complex and contradictory attitude to the beauty of this island and, by extension, to the land of his birth. In this house of many rooms, Barrie chooses a room where he 'can hide from the scenery' which he finds 'almost painfully' lovely.

Picturesque Outlooks

J. M. Barrie

13th August 1920

We have now been on the island a whole night, a wild rocky romantic island it is too, and if I had Michael of yours with me, as I do wish I had, we should have made great play of putting this in a bottle and letting it be picked up a la Crichton castaways. It might have reached you almost as soon, for the first five miles of its journey takes the better part of a day apparently as it lies at Acharacle a night before it sets out on the longer but easier part of its journey. You won't get it, I can see, before Sunday. Mothersil! I scorn your implication. All our sea-faring was on an inland loch as calm as the Serpentine and not much wider though there were a score or so of miles, and we had to stop now and again to get a bottle of milk from a rowing boat or give a sack of flour to another. All through the 'Pretender's' country – we lunched where he raised his standard and round about here he hid in caves when his sun went so quickly down. The sun has gone down for all who used to be great hereabouts – we look out on an aged keep where the last of the clan Ronald said farewell to his last acre.

This is a very lovely spot, almost painfully so. 'I am never merry' when I see sweet Scotia, or never merry any more, and have chosen a room where I can hide from the scenery. I should like to emerge with Simon in my arms, thus we could defy it together, laugh at it and still keep our feet. But for want of him I am better placidly peeping out on the rose garden to which I am still equal. It almost taketh the breath away to find so perfectly appointed a retreat on these wild shores. The Ritz could not do us better. Such bathrooms! Such a tennis court (the loveliest I should think in Britain – how could anyone with eyes let them rest for a moment on a ball!) Such boats. There is a tame lamb that would trot with Michael everywhere and lean against his legs when he stood still. Appliances to answer every thought. It is certainly a mighty fine present the Howard de Waldens have made us, or rather that you have passed on to us. Superb as is the scene from the door, Michael, who has already been to the top of things, says it's nought to what is revealed there – all the western isles of Scotland lying at our feet. A good spying ground for discovering what really became of Mary Rose. Speaking of her, it was all fixed up before I left London that Nesbitt should play Harry and Simon in U.S.A. He is in great feather, as his salary jumps from £8 or so a week to £50, but he doesn't know that this was done mainly to please you, as indeed it was. So please be rather elated.

Whereas J.M. Barrie lived in the island's mansion, Mike Tomkies lived in the island's shack and this seems to intensify his contemplation of loneliness, art and nature. This passage describes a profound turning point in the life of one of the great naturalist writers.

Finding the Pattern
Mike Tomkies

As usual I dreaded Christmas Day. When I woke to torrential rain I took refuge from my isolation by turning on the radio. There had been a record spending spree in Britain and holiday flights to the Mediterranean were double the previous year. A force 9 gale, 'imminent' in my area and nowhere else, was announced. Maybe the roof *will* blow off today!

Then followed one of those interminable pop music programmes with folk requesting DJs they didn't know to 'wish' love to husband, sister, wife, and names and addresses were reeled off as if from a phone directory. Bleating, nasal, reedy or cat-strangle-voiced singers followed one another in dreary succession, each one being called 'great' or 'wonderful' or 'superb' by the hosts who had more than a vested interest in perpetuating the slop. From one came a lyric 'People who need people are the luckiest people in the world'.

Not if they don't have anyone, they're not, I thought bitterly. In fact to me the precise opposite seemed to be the truth. Then for the first time I heard a song from a new rock musical about the life of Christ! The strange line 'Who do you think you are...' was bawled out by a crying female voice, presumably referring to Christ himself. Later some church minister was saying such musicals would lead to a revival of Christianity. What they will be is just more linchpins in further reducing the recorded life and example of the man-Christ, the truth he had lived unto death – that only love and creation-in-love redeem – to the level of another mere folk tale. To sheer away the superstitious symbols, props and dogmatic assertions clapped on later by the many often-profiteering churches was one thing, but to replace the brave subtle philosophy with slick sentimentality was no whit better. I turned the radio off for good that day.

In the silence that followed I felt increasingly lonely, but I wrote until near dark, then cooked a usual lunch, adding chips and lighting a few candles as my only concession to Christmas. As the chips crackled in the pan I realized I had been unconsciously preparing myself for the year-end holiday – refraining from drinking for a few days so I would have a little treat in store for Christmas itself. But now, as I sipped sherry and wine before eating, I realized I was acting from mere habit, forcing myself to enjoy in the traditional manner. With two half bottles gone I knew there was no point in drinking alone and put them away.

After lunch I wiped my sweatered arm over my records and put on the battery player my favourite Berlioz, Haydn, Mozart and Beethoven. Had not the great pianist Vladimir Horowitz been a recluse for twelve years too? I was alone with no loved woman at my side, but as the Eroica boomed through the croft from the wooden box in which I had set the tiny speaker, I recalled that many fine creators had been lonely men, often unsuccessful in their own lifetimes. Beethoven never married. Haydn's great love went off to a convent. Berlioz had disastrous love affairs. Bizet died before 'Carmen' was performed, never knowing of its success. Rembrandt died in poverty. Schubert made a mere £600 from his work during his lifetime. Van Gogh, whose paintings now fetch millions, sold only one in his lifetime (to his brother) and shot himself in despair.

The misunderstood Nietszche and the exquisite nature poet John Clare died in asylums. The rural morons about him called the great Richard Jefferies 'loony Dick'. Even Thoreau had died a failure at forty four having himself had to pay for some of his work to be published. But none of this seemed to me to be tragedy for I realized that all true creators have a reward which is denied to most – the joy of creation itself. Approval by others is merely the seal upon the treasure chest. It seemed to me the only real truth for an artist of any kind is to smile ironically at misfortune – and to keep trying.

Quite suddenly a memory of the actress Brigitte Bardot came into my mind. We had been talking for hours in her flat in the Avenue Paul Doumer in Paris in the early 1960s when I asked her if, in spite of her numerous romances, she ever felt lonely? She replied at length, and I now recalled the sad and serious expression on that dramatic face as she ended with 'Everybody is really alone. We are always alone. You are alone when you are born and you are alone when you die. All your life you are alone. To me it is normal.'

As I mused a small white moth suddenly leaped from a niche in the woodwork, flew wildly around, then with a brief 'whoff' burnt itself in the flame of the candle, and fell to the table beside me. It stayed there a moment, rearing up on front legs as if beseeching forgiveness, then it flew up again; hit the flame and sank on to its tail, its wings drawn back like an archangel's, its feet praying against the wick. Its long proboscis glowed red like hot coals and the whole body went dark as the wax spread up it. Then suddenly, with a little pop, it burst into flame and became part of the wick, flames now springing from its head. Poor moth! It could not resist the flame and so it had died before its time. While the rain sounded softly on the tin roof, almost in harmony with the fine music now filling the little room, I needed to take my mind away from negative musings and self-pity. I selected two new books I had bought by the writer I admired more than most, Henry Williamson. As I picked up the first I felt startled by its title, *The Dream Of Fair Women*. In the book Williamson's mystic, pantheistic, sensitive hero Willie Maddison retires from the horrors of war to a lonely Devon cottage to be at one with nature, and as I read Williamson's prose I found myself transfixed by his clear vision of beauty, of man and nature. For instance, he had Maddison write:

I can sympathize with all men because I am a man who wants natural happiness, someone to love, and someone to love me, to live with me in my cottage, to guard the well of my spirit where I draw Truth which is also my life. The day after I met you I sat here and loved the sun, the sea and the sky. Suddenly I was afraid; for I can love all these things but they do not respond. I realized that I should grow old, that I should die, and still the wind would shake the poppy, the blue butterfly seek the harebell, and trefoil be yellow on the hillside. I shall be gone, dead, and nothing I can do can avert that...

Even out of context I felt thrilled by passage after passage:

And certain idealists, whom men call fanatics and lunatics and criminals, try to break down the old civilization, hoping to recreate a better world of men but all is foredoomed to failure until the extra wisdom has come into men's minds. They neglect the secret of the woods and fields and how they expand man's spirit if he knows them when little...

I turned to the second book, *The Pathway*, realizing that his story of young Maddison was really confession on the part of one of Britain's greatest writers, yet one that has often been written off by effete intellectuals who do not understand what man has lost by severing himself too far from the natural world, who call him a mere 'nature writer'. I turned the pages again, finding more gems for my own heart:

I realized that all the world was built up of thought; that the ideals which animated the world were but thought, mostly mediocre and selfish thought. Change thought and you change the world.

I read on, surprised such words had been written in the early 'thirties, finding more passages that were so beautiful, so close to my own feelings and unpublished writings, I felt profoundly moved. It was as if Williamson was there with me, talking to me, his words giving me new strength. Suddenly I felt lonely no longer and it seemed there could be nothing more wonderful in the world than to sit there alone, a fire of gathered wood crackling behind me, reading such words. I was no longer unhappy for now I *knew* in my heart, really for the first time, that I was not withdrawing from reality, that loneliness was often the spiritual state of one who wished to create, successful or not. I would finish the commercial book before the old year was over and that would be farewell for ever to that kind of writing. As I rose to prepare supper, an odd thought came to me. In work I trust – all else is therapy.

Boxing Day dawned in a radiantly clear sky. For a while I worked on my book but when the sun streamed through the window after midday, I felt uncomfortable and went to look at the old ruined croft above. The storms had scattered the rotting boards over the ground, providing a fine source of new firewood, and I carried armfuls down to the croft.

I typed, on average, 5,000 words a day for the next four days before running out of carbons. By running the old ones over the top of the paraffin heater, so the remaining ink melted and spread itself over the surfaces, I was able to make ten more copies from each! On New Year's Eve, desperate to finish in time, I typed 14,000 words, a personal record of sheer, slogging work. I told myself I was just sitting there and tapping keys after all. It *had* to be done, no-one was going to help, and in the end sheer anger took me through. My stomach and back ached, my fingers felt weak across their backs, but by midnight I had the book beaten.

As the last words went down on paper Big Ben on the radio chimed in the New Year. While my pot of stew simmered away, I started flicking through the pages of a nature book I had bought on my last trip. To my surprise I could identify almost as many indigenous birds and butterflies as I could as a nature-loving boy. My glance fell upon the walnut sparrow hawk I'd lovingly carved at boarding school. Somehow it had stayed with me through all my travels and was now standing on the window shelf. Then I remembered something else and began to search among my boxes of forgotten books until I came to one wrapped carefully in plastic bags. It was a book about birds and butterflies I had written and painted in Sussex at the age of fifteen. My heart surged and for the first time in over 25 years everything seemed to fall into place in my mind.

The pattern had become crystal clear. Nature had been the one constant love throughout life. But it was no longer enough merely to enjoy the wilderness, use it as a retreat or for inspiration. I had to try and *pay it back*. It was then I made my one New Year resolution. From henceforth I would write only about nature and the last wild places and man's place in and influence upon them. I would finally abandon the novel and rewrite the Canadian wilderness book until it was the best I could possibly make it. That would be the indoor work while outside I would actively study the natural world in which I now found myself, the Scottish Highlands, one of the last truly wild areas left in Europe. Perhaps after 22 years of journalism, meeting man at his best and worst in half the western world, I could avoid the narrow, specialized naturalist's view. I knew now that only by giving myself totally to this new life, by trying to understand the magnificent Highland wilderness deeply, factually, and writing about it with reverence and love, had I the faintest chance of succeeding.

The decision made, I suddenly remembered my wise old Indian tracker in grizzly country, Pappy Tihoni, and how each New Year he slept out under the open skies in a symbolic act of spiritual renewal with nature. I took a double sleeping bag outside, into a world of violent indigo, the colour of ink, and there beneath the ash trees, waving their heads in the wind as if drowning, I slept peacefully until dawn.

Skye

In this letter to her artist sister, Virginia Woolf describes the vibrant colours of Skye – an island as alien to her as the South Sea Islands – in which 'sheep and Skye Terriers' are said to be the only industries.

Musical Tea Kettles

Virginia Woolf

Flodigarry Hotel, 25th June (1938)

Well, here we are in Skye, and it feels like the South Seas – completely remote, surrounded by sea, people speaking Gaelic, no railways, no London papers, hardly any inhabitants. Believe it or not, it is (in its way, as people say) so far as I can judge on a level with Italy, Greece or Florence. No one in Fitzroy Street will believe this, and descriptions are your abhorrence – further the room is pullulating and popping with Edinburgh tourists, one of whom owns spaniels, like Sally, but 'all mine are gun trained, the only thing they wont carry being hares' – so I cant run on, did you wish it. Only – well, in Duncan's highlands, the colours in a perfectly still deep blue lake of green and purple trees reflected in the middle of the water which was enclosed with green reeds, and yellow flags, and the whole sky and a purple hill – well, enough. One should be a painter. As a writer, I feel the beauty, which is almost entirely colour, very subtle, very changeable, running over my pen, as if you poured a large jug of champagne over a hairpin. I must here tender my congratulations to Duncan upon being a Grant. We've driven round the island today, seen Dunvegan, encountered the children of the 27th Chieftain, nice red headed brats: the Castle door being open I walked in; they very politely told me the Castle was shut to visitors, but I could see the gardens. Here I found a gamekeepers larder with the tails of two wild cats. Eagles are said to abound and often carry off sheep: sheep and Skye

Terriers are the only industries; the old women live in round huts exactly the shape of skye terriers; and you can count all the natives on 20 feet: but they are very rapacious in the towns, and its no use trying to buy anything, as the price, even of Sally's meat, is at last 6 times higher than in our honest land. All the same, the Scotch are great charmers, and sing through their noses like musical tea kettles. The only local gossip I've collected for you is about your Mr Hambro's wife – the one who was drowned in Loch Ness. We met a charming Irish couple in an Inn, who were in touch, through friends, with The Monster. They had seen him. He is like several broken telegraph posts and swims at immense speed. He has no head. He is constantly seen. Well, after Mrs Hambro was drowned, the Insurance Company sent divers after her, as she was wearing 30,000 pounds of pearls on her head. They dived and came to the mouth of a vast cavern, from which hot water poured; and the current was so strong, and the horror they felt so great, they refused to go further, being convinced The Monster lived there, in a hollow under the hill. In short, Mrs Hambro was swallowed. No drowned body is ever recovered and now the natives refuse to boat or to bathe. That is all the local gossip. And I will *not* describe the colour.

Eilean Bhan

The distinguished naturalist, John Lister-Kaye vividly describes his first visit to this small lighthouse island, (The White Island) situated between Skye and the Kyle of Lochalsh, where Gavin Maxwell moved after his house, famously described in 'Ring of Bright Water', had been burnt to the ground. Maxwell had ambitious plans to create an island zoo but he died before the project was realized. In the second passage, John Lister-Kaye reflects on the nature of island living.

An Island Is Essentially Different
John Lister-Kaye

I dumped my belongings down on the beach and sat on a large flat stone to await the boat from the island. The sea was calm and in places where no current ran it lay shimmering like glass. At its edge there was the gentlest movement, tiny wavelets lapping the shingle at my feet. The air was so still that I could hear the hum of the dinghy's outboard engine even before it left the island jetty. It appeared suddenly from behind the island promontory like a mouse from its hole and headed out into the seaway, a speck on the water with a curling white wake peeling away from its bow. The seaway was dotted here and there with little groups of guillemots and gulls which rose hurriedly to settle again well clear of the dinghy's path.

The beach shelved away quickly below me and I could see the transition from the crystal shallows at my feet to the vivid green of deeper water a few yards out. Down there I could see oar-weed and sea-tangle waving, an effortless, sinuous motion. The whole scene was so peaceful that with the warm sun on the back of my neck I was tempted to close my eyes and doze. I stood up and stretched and walked a little way down the beach. The island and its stout white sentry were reflected full length in the shimmering deeps at its foot, and behind it the imposing hulks of Raasay and Scalpay stretched dim and blue to the horizon. The sky was bright blue, the first I had seen for many weeks, and wisps of cirrus cloud hung like tufts of cotton wool. The impression after months of storm and wind ran deep and, although I have now seen this water lashed by a hundred-mile-an-hour gale into raging fury with fifteen-foot waves pounding in savage thunder against the lighthouse, that image of tranquillity remains in my mind.

The dinghy nosed on to the shingle beside me with a crunch and Andrew Scot, dressed in a home-made sealskin jacket, offered a greeting hand and a stout arm to take my luggage and help me climb inboard. Andrew was blunt and laconic and had a mop of dark shaggy hair. We had met before and beyond a greeting he saw no reason for idle chatter. We crossed to the lighthouse in silence. As we drew into the jetty beneath the lighthouse I realized that the low strip of the island which had been visible from Skye and the mainland was but a fraction of its whole area. Andrew secured the dinghy to her mooring and together we walked up the rabbit-cropped sward to the house.

Outside the house stood a long bench seat and a stout table. Gavin sat at the table, leaning forward with his eye to a small telescope on a tripod. The telescope pointed down on to the water directly in front of the island. I approached the table and put down my cases.

'Hello John,' he said still leaning over the telescope. 'So sorry not to greet you properly but there's ... aha! ... no, damn! it's a cormorant ... er ... as I was saying, there's a bird down there I rather want to see. It's dived at the moment but it should be up any moment now.'

'What is it?' I inquired as I unbuckled my field glasses.

'Well, I only caught a glimpse before it dived, but I think it's a white-eyed pochard. I do want you to see it otherwise no one'll believe me.'

'Isn't that the ferruginous duck?' I asked training my glasses on the water.

'Yes, that's it ... rare vagrant ... never seen one here before. Trouble is, with all these cormorants and shags bobbing up and down all over the shop it's the devil's own game to know what's what.'

'Aha!' We exclaimed in unison as a brown duck bobbed to the surface and shuffled its tail from side to side.

'That's him all right, can you see him clearly?' said Gavin.

'Yes, fine ... well I could, but he's dived again now.'

'Blast it, yes! So it has.'

We watched the duck for several minutes as it dived and surfaced until it swam out of sight behind one of the smaller islands in the archipelago. Then Gavin got up from the table and we shook hands.

'Hope you're going to enjoy your stay,' he said warmly.

'Well, if you can keep the weather like this and lay on ferruginous ducks to watch every day you might have trouble getting rid of me,' I said seriously. We went into the house.

The double doors led straight into the main room. It was a study and living-room combined, but it was known as the long room. Forty feet long and twelve feet wide with windows along the east wall, it looked out down the seaway between Kyle and Kyleakin. The room was dominated at the far end by an enormous Michael Ayrton, a wax and bone picture in low relief of Icarus falling from the sun with scorched wings. Below this framed work was a large natural stone fireplace, and two long Victorian sofas upholstered in silk brocade stood against the walls on either side. In the centre portion of the room beneath a large plate glass window stood a wide mahogany writing desk topped in red leather with gilt edging. This had been William Wordsworth's desk and was on permanent loan to Gavin. I had always thought of that room as a museum and although many of the exhibits were in everyday use, there were few items which had not some individual curiosity whether by virtue of their age, origin, beauty or rarity. The floor was carpeted throughout in a heavily patterned Indian weave and on top of the carpet were spread skin rugs. There were white and brown sheep fleeces, a goat skin, red and fallow deer hides and a hearth-rug made up from the furs of twenty fennec foxes. Around the walls hung a set of sixteen Thorburn water-colours of British game birds, and beside the fireplace were relics of a former venture, savage steel harpoons which were used to capture basking sharks when in 1945 Gavin started the Isle of Soay Shark Fisheries; a venture which, after years of tribulation and colossal expense, had finally to be abandoned. There were also souvenirs of long visits to Morocco where he wrote *Lord of the Atlas*, the dramatic history of the *House of Glaoua* and the tribe of the High Atlas Mountains; curved Moroccan daggers with jewelled hilts and silver sheaths, and primitive soapstone ware carved and decorated with simple dotted designs by the Berber tribesmen – bowls, boxes, jugs, saucers and ash-trays.

And there was also, inevitably, abundant evidence of his love of natural history. The pelt of an arctic fox hung beside the desk; the mantel shelf was cluttered with pebbles and shells intricately patterned by the serpulid worm; brilliant 'eye' feathers from a peacock's tail; two birds of prey skilfully mounted glared at each other across the room, and the framed fossil imprint of the famous *archeopterix* hung over the doorway to another room. The long room was a room for sitting and looking; it reflected the life of a fascinating man; it was a room thick with the atmosphere of travel and adventure and excitement. I found it difficult to sit there and talk about ordinary, everyday trivialities.

*   *   *

The early days passed quickly. Life on an island, however modern and well-equipped the living conditions, is essentially different. Above everything is the feeling of separation from the main body of civilization. In no part did that island belong either to the mainland community at Kyle or to Skye. It was separate, individual and aloof. The entire absence of every form of compulsion from any organizing establishment, and of every imposition of routine which one accepts as normal in a communal existence, was something I was not accustomed to, and it took a conscious effort to acclimatize myself. The island was well equipped for long periods of storm when it might not be possible to get a boat into or away from the jetty. The deep-freezes were well stocked with food and there were capacious fuel storage tanks which meant that daily trips to Kyleakin village, although often desirable, were not strictly necessary. In the event, it was found more convenient for Donald to cross to Skye every morning to collect Willie and again at night to take him back than to provide a separate dinghy for Willie's own use. While under different circumstances I would have been content to exist in a state of utopian isolation for days or even weeks at a time, it was clear that in order to get the construction of the zoo under way, some semblance of routine would be necessary. But it was a routine which was happily flexible and which destroyed none of the relaxing benefits of island life.

During those early days I underwent a complete mental reshuffle. For the first time in my adult life I found myself able to review a situation unhindered by consideration of position and status, to be idealistic without fear of scorn or rebuke, and to respond naturally to the demands of an existence free from pretence and devious motivation. I believe that only on an island like Kyleakin is it possible to experience this sort of entire reassessment of purpose and direction. The isolation must be monastic; and the distractions, if there must be distractions, must come not from human intervention but direct from nature.

Raasay

The great Gaelic poet, Sorley MacLean reflects on the influences of the island of his birth.

Words and Music

Sorley MacLean

Raasay, the island on which I was born, had great 'pibroch' playing about the end of the eighteenth century and the first half of the nineteenth from John MacKay and his sons, of whom Angus was the most famous; and great 'light' pipe music from two Donald MacLeods, one of whom survived well into the twentieth century, but was not living in Raasay in my time. Although my own father was rated a very fine piper, he seldom played 'pibroch', but used to be very enthusiastic about those he heard at the Portree Games. He could sing the 'Cro of Kintail' as if it were a pibroch, however, and with his voice make magic of what Iain Crichton Smith has called 'the infinite resonance that is in William Ross', the Skye/Gairloch poet. When my brother John and I used to go to Braes for the second half of August, we could hear much pibroch from the youngest of my mother's seven brothers, James Nicolson. James often played the gloriously melodic 'Lament for Mary McLeod', usually attributed to Pàdraig Og MacCrimmon.

Long before 1920-22, the years when I heard James in my boyhood, my earliest memories are of my paternal grandmother (nee Mary Matheson) singing some of the great 'sub-literary' songs, such as two of the five extant elegies for John Garve MacLeod of Raasay, who was drowned in 1671, and about whom there were innumerable legends. Most of the songs were that ineffable fusion of music and poetry, in which the melodies seem to grow out of the words and be a simultaneous creation. After my grandmother's death in 1923, her eldest daughter Peggy used to stay with us for about a month every year, and spend almost all her time fishing, for which she needed a crew. I, being then very keen on boats, was her most regular crew, but liable to threaten a strike if she would not sing. Peggy seemed to have even more songs than her mother, songs she had perhaps heard from her father, who died in 1889 when Peggy would be about twenty, and my father only nine or ten. He was reputed to be a bit of a singer and a bit of a bard. One of my mother's sisters lived in Braes and was often over in Raasay: she too had a good voice, a great memory and many old songs.

*   *   *

I was a pessimist. Looking back and around, I could see the miseries of the Industrial Revolution and the Clearances – in 1938 I was teaching in Mull, a heart-breaking place – and looking forward, the hopelessness of a Europe under the Nazis or Fascists of whatever kind. I don't think I had any particular ambitions as a poet, but I could hardly bear to think of a time when there was no one left with Gaelic enough to hear to the full the great song-poetry of our people, the 'fair, golden one' of the poem 'An Saothach' ('The Ship'), written as early as 1934. The 'black' one of that poem was the more or less professional Gaelic poetry that was not necessarily great song. Both were assailed by the Celtic Twilight, the Fundamentalist, and the 'Improver' – who was usually a Twilightist.

Of course, I was very often a symbolist of a kind. I think that was inevitable in one who came to maturity during the reigns of Eliot, MacDiarmid, Valery and Blok. Sometimes, as in 'Hallaig' and 'The Cuillin', the symbolism was double or even triple. William Ross had sometimes made 'sound poetry' as well as something else, and in 'The Tree of Strings' I tried to do the same. That is why the poem is curtailed somewhat in the present edition, for the more a poem approaches 'sound poetry', the more untranslatable it becomes.

'The Cuillin' is also a curtailed and somewhat revised version, because it was brought to a sudden end. Although I allowed Douglas Young to take it, it was never intended to be published without drastic revision. 1944 disgusted me with some of its politics, especially when Sydney Goodsir Smith convinced me that the behaviour of the Russian government at the time of the Polish insurrection was far worse than Professor Erikson's *Road to Berlin* now shows.

Up to the Second World War, there were in Raasay many of the native birches, hazels, rowans, elders and planted conifers of many kinds, and also a relatively large area of deciduous trees, beeches, chestnuts, elms, ash, oaks, thujas, aspens – even eucalyptus, planted by a wealthy English family of landlords from 1875 onwards. With the War they were nearly all cut down, and replaced by quick-growing conifers. I soon became very fond of the 'old woods' of Raasay, but I don't know at what age I became really appreciative of the varied scenery of the island, which is due to its great geological variety in a very small compass, and its wonderful position between Skye on the west, and Kintail, Lochalsh, Applecross and Torridon, from the south-east to the north-east. I did hear much about the Cuillins and the other hills of Skye from the eldest of my Nicolson uncles, Alexander, when I was about eight or nine. I suppose those glowing descriptions did something to enhance my later fascination with the contrast between 'the woods of Raasay' and the Cuillins, across the stretch of water called the Clàrach, the southern part of the Sound of Raasay. Between 1934 and 1937, when I was teaching in Portree High School, I did a great deal of ridge-wandering in the Cuillins, very often alone, and that enthusiasm replaced my boyish enthusiasm for boats.

It was in Mull in 1938 that I conceived the idea of writing a very long poem, 10,000 words or so, on the human condition, radiating from the history of Skye and the West Highlands to Europe and what I knew of the rest of the world. The long poem was always to me a *faute de mieux* as compared with the lyric, but I have come to regard it as a necessity if poetry is to deal with much of the human condition. By 'Lyric' I mean short poems like many Gaelic songs and the lyrics of Blake, Shelley and MacDiarmid. I think two of the reasons for my long silences and burning of unpublished poems have been my long years of grinding school-teaching and my addiction to an impossible lyric ideal. During my sixteen years at Plockton the burden of school-teaching was aggravated for myself by my starting the teaching of Gaelic there, and that to pupils who did not know it already.

In spite of MacDiarmid, the 'full-time' professional poet is not for me and never has been. If I have time to do it, I brood over something until a rhythm comes, as a more or less tight rope to cross the abyss of silence. I go on it, as far as I can see, unconsciously.

Over a period of some ten years, Calum MacDonald built a road, almost single-hand-edly, to his remote crofting township, out of sheer frustration at the interminable delays of local government. His road remains as a symbol of human defiance.

The Island of Strong Men
Roger Hutchinson

There are indeed no roads through the island, unless a few detached beaten tracks deserve that name.

James Boswell, Journal of A Tour to the Hebrides, 1773

On a spring morning in the middle of the 1960s a man in his fifties placed into his homemade wooden wheelbarrow a pick, an axe, a shovel and a lunchbox. He trundled this cargo south from his crofthouse door, down a familiar, narrow, rutted bridle path, up and down rough Hebridean hillsides, along the edge of hazardous cliff-faces, through patches of bent and stunted hazel and birch and over quaking peat bogs.

After almost two miles he stopped and turned to face homewards. Before him and to his left were steep banks of bracken, turf, birch and hazel. To his right, green pastureland rolled down to the sea. There were sheep on this pasture, and, close to the shore, a small group of waist-high stone rectangles which once, a century ago, had been the thatched cottages of a community called Castle. The vestigial masonry of a medieval keep teetered on an outstanding crag a few yards from the deserted home-steads, melding into the bedrock so naturally that, 500 years after they were first erected and 300 years since they were last occupied, it had become difficult to tell from a hundred yards away where the remnant walls of the man-made fortress finished and the natural stone began.

Then, alone in an empty landscape, he began to build a road.

He started by widening his workspace. He cleared the scattered clumps of wind-blasted native woodland which lay on either side of the old track. He chopped the dwarf trees down, and then he dug up their roots. He gathered the detritus carefully into piles at the edge of his planned route. He worked a long day. He was accustomed to working long days.

And at the end of that first long day, when he reassembled his equipment in the wheelbarrow and began his walk home, he had denuded several yards of ground. He had, in fact, accomplished slightly more than one thousandth of a task which would take him twenty years to complete, which would pay him not a material penny and would cost him little more, but which would leave his manifesto marked in stone upon his people's land.

His name was Calum MacLeod. He belonged to the township of South Arnish in the north of the island of Raasay.

*   *   *

Even the wind would rarely stop Calum working. He worked, as all of his people had always worked, through the worst and the best of weather. He worked hunched up against the storm, bent by the gale, chilled by the cold, sweating in the unaccustomed sun, soaked by unpredicted showers of sleet – sometimes all on the same day. The weather would never defeat him. The weather would change and go elsewhere. Calum MacLeod would not.

If Calum was indefatigable, the same could not be said of his tools. He was, on one occasion, levering a large rock out of the hillside over his road. His crowbar took purchase of it and the boulder began to move. It rolled out of the hollow in which it had stood since the Jurassic Age, tumbled down the slope, struck the road, bounced once and landed on top of his wheelbarrow, spatchcocking it to the ground. In total Calum worked his way through three wheelbarrows, six picks, six shovels, five sledgehammers, four spades and one crowbar while building the road between Brochel Castle and Arnish. It was estimated that the largest single boulder he removed weighed nine tons. It stood in the path of his road. He used a jack to lift it, then packed it in place with stones, then jacked it up again, then repacked it with stones, then jacked it once more ... until it had been heaved out of his way and had fallen, defeated, into the sea. He was accompanied on his painstaking travail between Brochel Castle and Arnish by a tiny portable storage hut which edged its way, yard by yard, month by month, year by year, along the verge in line with Calum's progress.

Having animals to milk and feed, and other crofting chores to complete, Calum MacLeod could not spend all of every working day on the road. His early attempts to keep track of the hours through modern time-keeping devices failed, as one wrist- or pocket-watch after another was smashed during his heavy manual labour. So he resorted to a basic portable sundial. This was no more than a stick put upright into the ground. 'It was surprisingly accurate', said his daughter. 'He would return home with a half-hour margin of error. And it fascinated his grandchildren!'

Barra

With her remarkable combination of practical wisdom and mystical attachment to the land, Margaret Leigh was one of the finest British rural writers of the 20th century and here she describes a place where 'the dead are buried on the edge of wild ocean'.

Graves On The Machair

Margaret Leigh

It was at midnight, and in winter, that I first set eyes on the isle of Barra. We crossed the Minch in storm and driving rain; but soon after leaving Lochboisdale the wind died away, and we made our landfall under clearing skies and on a sea whose black and polished surface reflected the harbour beacons. The *Lochearn* stole past the shadow of Muldoanich, wallowing in the long swell that rolled in from the Atlantic through the narrows of Vatersay. Save for a glimmer from the canvas-screened bridge, the upper deck was in darkness: the mast-head lamp swung in a wide slow arc among the stars. Ahead, under the lowering mass of Heaval, were the clustered lights of Castlebay, with its houses and curing sheds, and high on the rock the church of Our Lady, Star of the Sea. As we drew alongside the pier, the sheen from the lamps fell on a host of upturned faces, eager, expectant, for no one goes to bed without seeing the boat come in. I went ashore under the wing of one of those commercial travellers of the isles who ply their trade precariously in rowing-boats and in pony-traps, and can tell, over a cup of strong stewed tea, tales that have a faint but authentic flavour of the Arabian Nights. Next day, in return for his kindness, I went to the village hall and helped him to arrange a show of Glasgow boots and shoes, not one of which was suited to the rocks and bogs of the Western Isles.

It was later on a Sunday afternoon that I discovered the fittest if not the most beautiful burial-ground in the world. It was one of those wild, brilliant north-westerly days that follow a great gale. A stiff breeze was still blowing, with an occasional rattle of hail from hard-edged anvil-head-ed clouds. Between showers the February sun was warm, and I scrambled along the rocky southern fringe of Halaman bay in a vain attempt to pho-tograph the immense breakers that were rolling in upon the sands. When I had gone far enough to see round and over the northern horn of the bay, I caught sight of a further promontory flung far into the ocean, and at its extremity a walled enclosure full of headstones and crosses. It was more than a mile away in a direct line, and separated by an expanse of heaving green water, laced and marbled with foam, over which the shin-ing crests of waves chased one another shoreward, and the noise that went up drowned every other sound. Turning back, I skirted Bachd and crossed the mouth of the glen that holds the crofting townships of Borve and Craigston. Here I left the road and walked across the short turf towards the burial-ground. The point on which it stood was low, and fringed with shelving rock, and the brilliant green grass came to the level of the high spring tides. There were some Barra ponies grazing near, dun, strongly built, with flowing manes and tails, and a few cross-bred sheep, some with lambs, for spring comes early to the sea pastures. The Ordnance Survey marks the site of a chapel of St. Brendan the Navigator, but at that time I could find no trace of the ruins. They lie close above a little cove on the southern side, where the coracles beloved of Irish saints could have found a landing.

The sagging gate, secured with a bit of string, left plenty of room for the traffic of sheep, and I was not surprised to find a ewe inside, resting under the lee of the wall, and her lamb playing among the graves. And who would put them out, for these walls are the only shelter on the whole windswept promontory, and the grass within is rich and sweet. The grave-stones, old and new alike, were weathered to one grey, tufted with lichen, encrusted with salt, as if coeval with the rocks on which they stood. The sun, shooting out from a retreating hail-cloud, lay warmly on the place, and I sat down for a while beside the ewe, who did not trouble to move. At the little church on the edge of the sands, people were coming out from Benediction, the older ones in their Sunday blacks, the younger in clothes more modern. But these distant figures, dispersing up the glen or along the shore, soon dwindled or vanished; and all sounds of man or beast were swallowed up in the vast annihilating roar of the sea.

I looked over the parapet of the west wall, with the salty tang of spray on my lips, and saw nothing but tumbling green water, and a smother of snow-white foam, and shining clouds piled on the sharp horizon. Fifty miles out, at that low level invisible, was the lonely Isle of St. Kilda, in Gaelic called Hirta, which is said to be an ancient word for death, and beyond that the empty wastes of ocean. Later, I thought, the sun will go down in cloud-banks and trailing showers, and this burial-ground, with its freight of memories and prayers, will slowly sink into darkness and the dead be left alone with the sea, now and for ever. A race of seamen, who in merchantmen and trawlers, in smacks and battleships, have given so many lives to the deep, might want to be buried in some sheltered glen where the noise of the surf is no more than a murmur, or at least in a place that faces the quieter waters of the Minch, and the sun rising over the kindly hills of the mainland. But no: for not only in Barra, but in other western isles, the dead are buried on the edge of wild ocean, as if there were some special grace in the nearness of the sea that was at once their field of labour, their grave, and their symbol of eternity.

South Uist

The Hebridean islands with their piercing clarity of light inspired many of Winifred Nicholson's most beautiful paintings. In this wonderful letter, she perceives almost every object, every creature and every islander in terms of dazzling colour as though each one was lit from within.

Like Chinese Singing

Winifred Nicholson

Isle of South Uist, [1950?]

Dearest Andrew,

This is the place after my heart. I wonder if you would like it. Not a tree, not a bush. But grey boulders, grey rocks, grey stones, grey mountains, and bog in between. In the bog, lochs with water lilies and rare ferns that love the black peaty soil. The sea full of grey mysterious islands and rocks, seals and seabirds. White glistening beaches and transparent sea all the way across to Eriskay. Blue mountains of Barra to the west, and the Cuillins far away snow covered to the south. There are five other cottages in Glendale and no road nearer than 3 miles. One comes by boat and then walks. The family consists of a father and mother, crofters, and sailor sons, and a daughter who goes to college in Glasgow, and an adopted orphan – everyone sings, everyone talks Gaelic. There are 2 collies, 3 puppies, 2 black cats, 4 cows, 3 calves, innumerable hens and cocks and chickens, and the point is to try to keep them out of the cottage.

Peat fire, water carried from a well, everything as primitive as you want. Everyone spins, dyes wool with wonderful dyes from lichens, yellow iris root, water lily root, blue or peat fire soot which makes yellow, and thus weaves into beautiful tweed.

This croft has this tiny white cottage on a rock, 2 rooms and 3 attics. It has a minute meadow by the stream, all kingcups, ferns, orchids, and ragged robin, a small cow pasture all yellow iris, two thousand acres of bog and mountain – for which it pays £3 a year, and seems to just subsist on it, if all the men go to fish and to be sailors, and the girls make tweed. Everyone is happy.

Over about 2 miles of bog, there are 2 old ladies who live in a one-roomed white cottage, thatched. They have a wonderful white calf, and a red duck, the room is full of fleeces drying after the dying. They can make a crotal dye from lichen off the rocks that is browner and purpler than anyone else, and O what wonderful songs they sing, with this queer Hebridean cadence and modes that sound like Chinese singing. They are both very small like fairy women, and the walls of their house are 4 feet thick – and they have soft white hair like silk and they are almost bent double with old age and their eyes are bright blue and O, the laughter and the jokes they make.

We went to church at Eriskay on St Peter's day, everyone is a Catholic, over in the boat to Eriskay. All the men in sailor's navy blue jerseys and the women in black with wonderful shawls over their heads, knitted by themselves in strange patterns.

I have painted 9 pictures and enjoyed myself bathing and basking on the warm sand. It has rained once, and the sun has shone gold and the sea has glittered blue each day and every day. All the work runs very smoothly and easily. Kathleen [Raine] has written some good poems, and I have made friends with a lot of wild seabirds, watching them fly and soar and sink on to the sea – the great black-backed gulls are tremendous fellows even carrying off lambs, the eider ducks are very charming and talk in confidential tones, the oystercatchers are brave and chase the great black-backed gulls away when they come to steal their eggs. There are hundreds of darting sand martins that nest in burrows on the river's banks. Ravens in the crags to the right of us, buzzards nest in the crags to the left, and the Lighthouse Island is full of arctic terns – the most graceful and beautiful of all. Kathleen saw a whale spouting in Loch Hourn, and I saw some chicks of the sandpipers lying on the shingle and pretending to be dead until I took my eye off them and then the family scuttled to the next large stone.

Love to you, from Mother

In 1954 the distinguished American photographer, Paul Strand spent three months on the three South Uist islands (which also include Benbecula and Eriskay) and created unforgettable black and white images of the islanders and their stark and beautiful land. Here, Catherine Duncan writes with deep perception of these photographs.

Moments Outside Time

Catherine Duncan

The photographs impose reflection, like a sudden stillness when everything stands on the edge of discovery. It is the hour of midday when the clock folds its hands or lays them palm downwards on the knees of an old woman resting on peat cut and stacked, wool spun and dyed, children and grandchildren. It is the moment when a man pauses to look across the fields of his inward years, marked out by crops and haystacks, sheep to be shorn and pastured. It is the boat tied up, and ropes and lobster pots drying, the sudden watchfulness of children before the unknown, the shaggy, stocky cattle daydreaming in the heather.

For those who live them such moments are outside time, when the view is detached from the surface of things and restores to them their essential meanings. Then these islands, pressed between the sides of sea and sky, yield up the most microscopic of their secrets. Nothing is nonessential or unrelated. Nothing is simply what it seems.

Paul Strand presses into the texture of stone and wood, cloth and wood, plant and pottery, elucidating the tactile messages of their substance, seeking within them the hidden explanation of their endurance and renewal. They are not merely objects, but the very stuff of people, the foundations on which they rest. Set in their context, the heads of these men and women, of their children, might be frescoes drawn on the granite, which lends its character to their flesh and blood.

But the faces have their private depth. One is reminded of the old daguerreotype and the long pose with its slow melting away of the sitter's Sunday face. These portraits have an inward contemplation, a dignity which establishes equality between the observed and the observer. It is as if the camera has recorded the long impression of growth and change, of habit and social practice, which has gone into the making of their personalities. One might match them with the doors and windows Paul Strand has always liked to photograph, these openings which look out and lead inward.

Scattered and solitary houses – small holdings on a spare and stubborn soil – a derelict boat – a tangle of seaweed, but in Paul Strand's world there is an order which exists, more perhaps in the will and determination of its people than in the apparent reality. Over the centuries a pact has been established between the rocky earth of the Hebrides and its crofters and fishermen. The terms of this pact are based on the solidarity between man and his material universe. They are partners in the hard fact of existence. The dry tough roots which writhe out of rock and sand take a new sap from men's palms when they are turned into the handles of spades and pitchforks or walking sticks. There are flowers everywhere, in window-pots and lace curtains. Knitted into woollens – wild iris and heather, daisies and pansies, the floral prints of aprons and children's frocks. A drowned boot is washed up in flowers of kelp.

A tar-pot can speak for a man, and a horse's skull for the dead. Rocks bear down the roof-thatch against the winds which lift the thatch of hair on a boy's head. The grass bends but holds like a bull's pelt. Over the sound of surf one hears the proud skirl of pipes and the thin reedy songs of ancient bards.

In the kitchen, while the woman is absent, china dogs and tea caddies stand guard over pots and kettle whispering on the stove. The dresser bears a testimony of eggcups, plates, whisky bottles, and holy pictures – what Cocteau called a 'carousel of silences', in which the whole family is engaged.

Paul Strand has given us images of the old, old hope of all those marooned on the Outer Hebrides of our times. His photographs are not the trompe l'oeil of an eternal and repetitive pattern of existence, but a heightened realism which claims that what is presented as fixed and immobile can still be changed, the pact renewed, and man participate in the orphic mysteries of his world.

Harris

Bill Lawson memorably describes the often tragic history of this hauntingly beautiful island as if witnessed by the ancient standing stone which stands above 'a pure white Atlantic shell-beach' and has watched dispassionately over the island and its people for some five thousand years. Here we read of the events of the past three hundred years or so. We read not only a factual account but of the perhaps deeper truths of poetry and myth.

MacLeod's Stone

Bill Lawson

The Stone remembered some of the great gatherings in the early 1700s, when MacLeod of Harris had gathered all his tenants together to pay their rent and to renew their leases. The settlement pattern then was very different from that of today. The modern centres of An Tairbeart and an t-Ob were merely a few houses on the shores, the rugged east coast, the Bays, was virtually empty, and the population was concentrated on the west machair shore, the offshore islands, a few sheltered spots among the hills of North Harris, and around the religious centre of Roghadal.

The main centres of population were on the islands – Pabaigh, Bearnaraigh and Tarasaigh – where the land is more fertile than on the mainland, and on the machair strip running from Taobh Tuath to Losgaintir. Each village, in addition to its own town-lands, had a grazing area for airighean, or summer shielings, and these occupied most of the Bays, and large tracts of the North Harris hills, among which were also located the homes of the foresters, or gamekeepers of MacLeod's deer-forest.

These villages were largely self-supporting, with some trade in small black cattle. In contrast to today, there were only a few sheep, but there was much more growing of small oats and bere. Bearnaraigh, Tarasaigh and Roghadal had good natural harbours and fishing was a year-round occupation there. But the Atlantic exposed shores of the machair on either side of the Stone had no harbours, and the people there had to rely on summer fishing in their shieling lands in the Bays.

In 1779 Harris had been sold to Captain Alexander MacLeod of Berneray. He reckoned that the fishings of Harris could be changed from a seasonal activity to a full-scale industry. This could only be done on the Bays side of the island, with its hundreds of little bays facing the Minch, so he constructed a harbour at Roghadal, and set up fishing stations all up and down the Bays. Some of the people of the machair and the islands had moved to these new villages but many of the new settlers were from Lewis, Uist and Skye, together with masons, boatbuilders etc. brought in from the mainland. Captain MacLeod's experiment worked well for a few years but after his death, much of the impetus was lost.

But already a new industry had appeared, which provided unheard-of income for the islands, and in the end ruined their economy. This was the period of the French Wars, and with overseas markets closed to Britain, there was an unprecedented demand for minerals, many of which could be derived from the ash of kelp, or seaweed. The Bays and Islands of Harris were ideally suited for the collection and manufacture of kelp, and the whole economy of the island was changed to one based on the value of the seaweed. More and more people were encouraged to settle on barren shores, where they could not possibly feed themselves from the land – but that did not matter so long as there was employment on the kelp. The landlord had of course got most of the profits, but there had been plenty left over to buy food and to pay the rents, which had been increased to take account of the value of the weed on the shore. Even on the machair, the kelp cast ashore by the Atlantic storms had been gathered and burned, instead of being used for manure on the land – the Stone could remember the choking clouds of acrid smoke coming from the burning kelp.

After the wars came the inevitable crash. The continental markets were open again, and could produce better and cheaper minerals than could be got from kelp-burning. The price for kelp plummeted, and landlords and tenants alike lost their main source of income. Captain

Macleod's son and grandson had become society gentlemen on the strength of the kelp boom, and when it burst, it was reckoned that they lost three-quarters of their income. Unfortunately, like most Highland proprietors, they looked to their estates to replace their lost income. Rents were increased quite beyond the ability of the tenants to pay, despite the fact that they too had lost as great a proportion of their income.

Most of the landlords in the Highlands and Islands left the management of the estates to factors, and on Harris control of the estate was given to Donald Stewart, a sheep-farmer. His idea of a solution to the problem was to evict the crofters from every worthwhile bit of land, and to let it to a sheep-farmer. The Stone remembered the clearance of nearby Horgabost and Nisabost, some of the first villages to be cleared in Harris – it had been strange to have the land around its feet grazed by sheep, where there had once been cultivation, and the noise of people.

After the collapse of the kelp industry, many of the Harris crofters could see only too clearly what the future held. Those on the better lands were conscious of the threat of the expanding sheep-farms, and those on the kelp-shores could see no future but ever-increasing rents, with no income to pay them, and more and more people crowded on to the already insufficient land.

Cape Breton was being laid out for settlement at this time in the 1820s, and hundreds of families decided to emigrate and settle there, mainly around St Anns and Baddeck. When the Clearances began in earnest, the evicted people also went to Cape Breton, but since much of the better land had already been taken up, they tended to settle on the higher, poorer, land behind the coastal settlements, in areas like the North Shore, or at Loch Lomond and Grand River in south-eastern Cape Breton.

By the 1840s, there were no people left on the machair except a few sheep-farmers and their servants. For miles on either side of the Stone where there had been busy villages, there was now the desolation of the sheep farms, many of them run by Stewart and his own relatives.

Matters had become even worse with the advent of potato blight in the 1840s. In most of the bays, the potato was the only food crop which could be grown on the poor land, and when that failed, there was no choice left but either emigration or destitution. Hundreds of families left from this area too, but by this time the potato blight was in Cape Breton also, so the destination of the emigrants changed to Australia, with the financial assistance of the Highland and Islands Emigration Society.

The government was eventually forced to pay attention to the distress of the crofters, and the Napier Commission was set up to investigate the causes and possible cures for this distress. The Commission visited Harris in 1882, and the evidence given before them is a valuable record of the history of Harris. The Commission recommended a limited degree of security of tenure for crofters, and after the passing of the Crofters Act in 1883, much of the harassment of crofters by factors ceased.

In the early 1900s, the Congested Districts Board supervised the setting up of new crofting villages at Taobh Tuath and at Borgh in Bearnaraigh, while the Department of Agriculture sponsored a move to Portnalong and Fiskavaig in Skye and to the Lock Portain area of North Uist. After the First World War, the Department acquired the machair farms and resettled them as crofting townships. Once again the Stone could hear the sounds of people working their crofts – and if the sound was that of tractors instead of the horses of the old days, well – that was progress!

But the Stone also knows another story about its own origin – the one the old people told. Long ago, before the time of history, there was a Cailleach in Harris. The Gaelic word Cailleach means an old woman, but in this sense it means specifically a witch – and a fearsome witch she must have been! She was very fond of limpets – and if you have ever tried gathering limpets, you will know how difficult it is to dislodge them from their rocks. So the Cailleach had a stone hammer to knock the limpets off the rocks, and she wandered the shores, gathering her limpets. On Aird Nisabost she saw a particularly large one, and gave it a sideways hit with the hammer. Nothing happened! Another blow, and still nothing happened! Gathering all her strength the Cailleach gave a third blow to the limpet, which flew off the rock into the sea, But the hammer broke into three pieces with the force of the blow, the smaller parts going flying across the sea, one to land on the island of Tarasaigh and the other along the shore of Sgarasta, and the largest part landing on the hill behind her, where it is still known as the Ord Bhairnich – the Limpet Hammer.

And there you have the two types of story we can tell about Harris. Some are based on historical fact, but others are yarns heard around the fireside. Some are true, and others might not be, but they are all well worth telling!

The distinguished American travel writer, David Yeadon lived for a year on Harris and he writes of the vital, spiritual importance of doing nothing but attending to the world around you: something perhaps more readily done on a remote island.

Dawdle Days In The Dunes
David Yeadon

Alec Guinness once wrote: "Paying attention to anything is a window into the universe," and in our case we started off by paying attention just to the clouds. They alone are enough to occupy hours of observation as their profiles and moods change. Bold, bulging cumuli, massing across the horizon, tumescent, pearlescent, some cut by canyons, others puffy as soufflés or cuddly as plump cherubs under feathery brushstrokes of cirrus; a thunderhead growing over a sun-shafted summit and purpling under a flattening head – glowing with power as if barely containing its furies within.

Gulls fly close (I'm always surprised by their impressive size) and glide to smooth landings alongside one last tidal stream meandering its diminishing way across the beach to where the surf breaks gently on a distant strand. Two hours ago the surf was clearly visible in white-maned lines of waves, but with the tide receding, they barely exist now. It looks as if you could set off and walk straight across the three miles of sand to Taransay Island. It's a tempting proposition, just to head off in a straight line across those infinities of soft shell dust and see how far you could get before the tide decided it's time to turn again.

So we walk together slowly out in a wide arc across the sand and a great calm settles over us.

"We are so lucky," Anne said softly as if to avoid disturbing the silence and the gentle rhythm of our steps.

I nod and smile and know exactly what she means. Back in our small beach cottage, perched on a rocky buckle of land, we love everything. We need for nothing at all. We have our favourite music on a handful of CDs, a dozen or so "important" books we've been meaning to read for eons, a well-stocked refrigerator, a change of clothes, a guitar, notebooks and journals, a comfortable double bed, a couple of elephantine armchairs and a small but idyllic glass-enclosed sunroom overlooking the whole glorious vista of sand, dunes, mountains, and ocean. And then, of course we have time itself – time for thinking, daydreaming, looking, focussing, and letting free-floating feelings roll – a month's sensation and thoughts in a single day. And we have as well a sense of that "wild, roving, vagabond life" so celebrated by Sir Richard Burton, the famous Victorian explorer.

And rhythms. We have the slow, regular rhythm of the day, each and every day. Sometimes placid and predictable as the tides. Sometimes typically Hebridean, when, in the course of a single hour, we might watch the following sequence: first, a furious little rainstorm whirling in off the Atlantic on air currents that have crossed over those three thousand miles of untrammelled ocean; then angry little black clouds appearing over Taransay as if to express frustration at this unexpected island obstacle; and the rain coming at us across the sand, flailing like a horse's tail, hitting the large windows of our sunroom hard as hail. Taransay vanishes, lost in a sudden white mist-sheen. Then the whole bay vanishes and all we can see, through the rain-streaked glass, are small clusters of machair wildflowers a few feet away from the cottage, flailing about like placard-hoisting protesters at an anti-something-or-other rally.

I remember a comment Roddy had made a few days previous as one autumn storm too many had disturbed his normally calm demeanour: "Did y'know, David, that it's estimated there's more'n ninety billion gallons of rain falling on Scotland in an average year. An' I reckon most of it came down in the last two weeks ... directly on top of our wee island."

This time the petulant storm barely lasts three minutes. And then it's all over. The misty strands evaporate like wraiths suddenly exposed to daylight. And light comes. A watery sun at first, limpidly silver, then turning more and more sauterne-gold as the land appears once again. The long dune-strand of Corran Seilibost, the great concave profiles of the Luskentyre dunes, the languorous green profile of Taransay, and, still a little hazy, the bold bulk of the North Harris hills. They're all back in barely a minute with only our rain-dappled windows as evidence of the fickle storm fury.

And then comes the rainbow. Actually, this time it's one of those magnificent double rainbows – two perfect concentric arcs with each spectrum colour distinct and separate. And it's now warm again with the sun beaming in brazenly through the large sunroom windows. The sands gleam like burnished bronze, but down farther to the south, over the straggled croft community of Northton, another dark little storm suddenly appears atop Chaipaval and we watch the rain fall in silky white strands like long man-of-war tentacles.

As we turn eastward, looking through the living room windows, across the peaty wastes of the island's central spine, huge cumuli float like bulbous galleons toward the soaring cliffs of Skye. And to the north, over Clisham, shafts of sun burst through the mountains' semipermanent cloud cover and dapple the dun green-brown slopes with patches of emerald and polished copper hues. And finally, looking straight out at Taransay again, the rainbow is fading and – would you believe – another little petulant flurry of gale and rain look to be forming once more as the Atlantic air decries the arrogant intrusion of land . . .

Scalpay

In his travels in the Outer Hebrides in the 1930s, Louis MacNeice set out to adopt a detached, amused, ironic tone but one feels nevertheless that he was, at times, beguiled by the beauty of the landscape and the distinctive people he encountered.

To Strangers

Louis MacNeice

I was sent on to the end of the village where an old man rowed me over to Scalpay in a very heavy boat, rowing with long oars. He asked four shillings for the crossing which was a distance of about a hundred yards. I clambered up from the rocks on which I landed, up a steep hill of grass bastioned with naked peat, and came in sight of the houses which are grouped round two long harbours. I passed the skeleton of a steamboat with its bows run up the shore and walked along diffidently, wondering where to ask for a night's lodging. This was easier to find than I had expected. The woman of the house was at first rather eager to send me back to the mainland but gave way after ten minutes' conversation. I sat down in the kitchen and talked to her husband.

The nations of the world, he said, were in for a bad time. Scalpay, too, was not what it was. There used to be four or five curing stations on Scalpay but the herring fishing was nothing here now. He remembered when the German Klondikers used to come into Loch Seaforth and buy from the natives on the spot. Now there was no work for the young men and they had to go away into the Merchant Service.

He was very interested in the Jews whom he greatly admired. In the old days there were several Jews came round the islands. By the end of six months the Jews could speak Gaelic marvellously. Einstein was a Great Jew. He had read his theory in Gaelic in the Church of Scotland Magazine but could not make head or tail of it.

Scalpay has a population of from six to seven hundred, no horse and practically no road. They were, I was told, given a grant for a road for a year or two, but the grant was discontinued. The road now ends in the air above a potato field. A very stony track leads eastward connecting the houses, a number of which are Black Houses. The lobsters which are caught on Scalpay are all kept alive in a concrete pool, and sold for fancy prices at Christmas. I missed seeing the lobster pool, but I saw the lighthouse at the easterly point of Scalpay, reached by walking across the moors. I looked into one of the modern flat-roofed dwellings attached to the lighthouse (which had assumed inside the atmosphere of a croft) and was greeted by a young man who took me up the tower. The tower has a hundred and twenty-one steps and the light is 350,000 candle-power. The former fact means more to me than the latter. It occurred to me, as I admired the glass lantern, cut in diagonals and bulls' eyes, that a lighthouse tower is the best modern approximation to the towers in fairy stories where princesses are imprisoned. For lighthouses are round and narrow and painted outside in stripes. A hundred and twenty-one steps and you come to a crystal chamber, which can even revolve. If I was filming one of those fairy-stories I should certainly use a lighthouse.

From the top of this lighthouse is an excellent view of the Highland mainland, and Skye with the Shiant Isles dominating the nearer sea. Looking to the left from Scalpay you can see Loch Seaforth which divides the hostile territories of Harris and Lewis, and the steep hump of a mountain called Toddun.

I stumbled back across the moor, leaping the wet patches of bog while admiring the pink lousewort which grows there. I met a man with a long bamboo rod going to fish for lithe. I also met an old man sitting on the ground with his cat. 'A Norwegian cat', he said proudly. Its father had come off a Norwegian boat that ran aground and took to going with the island cats. When I reached my house it was ten o'clock and they made me some tea in the kitchen. There was an open fire burning in the built-in range – the range framed with green tiles, on the mantelpiece two large China spaniels and an old fashioned clock whose pendulum could be seen swinging lazily. Also a large dresser and a framed text. For my tea I had two boiled eggs – boiled for three minutes – some very good scones, home-made oatcakes, and a large hunk of 'crowdy' the size of an ostrich egg. Crowdy is a kind of very crumbly cream cheese, pure white and with practically no taste; I had had it before in Shawbost.

I went to bed at half-past ten – a very unusual experience, and found that, though I am only five-foot eleven, the bed was much too short for me. I had a long night as breakfast was not till half-past ten next morning. Next morning was Sunday. Bacon and eggs; more scones. They told me that a motor-boat had come from Tarbert to take some of the islanders there to hear a sermon by the Moderator, and that I could get a lift on it when it was mended, for something had gone wrong with it. One or two of the people from Tarbert came in and were most warmly greeted by my hosts. The people of Harris seem demonstratively affectionate and tend to clasp hands and kiss. They all spoke Gaelic to each other with great rapidity and expression – in great contrast to their manner of speaking English. As my host said to me, 'We get a bit rusty in the English. We never speak it except to strangers.'

Scarp

Anna Adams and her family kept returning to Scarp for holidays long after the island had been abandoned by its few remaining inhabitants. She finds, contrary to fashionable opinion, that human presence can actually enhance the environment.

We Are Good For Nature

Anna Adams

I can remember thinking, when the island community left, "Well, at least it will be good for the botany;" but this has not been so. The human race gives itself a bad press lately. We have taken to regarding ourselves as the blight of Earth; but I would like to defend us. In moderation we are very good for nature, and for landscape, but this opinion may be simply the result of the onset of middle age and deteriorating vision. Certainly I am no longer the romantic who used to like nothing better than a rip-roaring wilderness. I now like gardens. The world is just jungle and tangle and desolation without them. I even, sometimes, have a nostalgia for suburbs, but this is cured instantly, the moment I set foot in one. Nevertheless, I can now understand those islanders, marooned in the stone-age, with doctors and dentists miles away across seas and mountains, and whose lifelong efforts could achieve only subsistence, craving the easier life of cities and suburbs, where nature is kept in place, and where there are possibilities to develop other talents than backbending. Scarp was scarcely the land of opportunity.

I thought, though, that it might become the land of opportunity for plants; but I was wrong. The botany is actually impoverished by the cessation of human habitation and cultivation, and – perhaps – by the absence of cows. There used to be certain fields that, during the years when they were left to lie fallow, grew a nodding crop of scarlet poppies beside the glittering sea. Other places grew corn-marigolds in such profusion that they seemed like a patch of sunlight in a clouded landscape.

Heartsease also grew on fallow fields, and an ultramarine vetch scrambled about in the grass of hayfields. There were various sorts of large, yellow-centred, white daisies. These have all disappeared; only a remnant of the heartsease still remains, dwindling year by year. One reason for this is that certain plants like to have the soil turned over for them. They do not keep on reappearing in an undisturbed mat of turf. Another reason is that now that no one is cultivating, the sheep, which are still grazing Scarp's pasture, have things almost entirely their own way. There are no gardens to be protected, no hayfields to grow tall, so the sheep are pushed outside the village fence very late, and let in again in mid-August. So such flowers as primroses, persistently nibbled down until late June, only manage to flower in July and August. Harebells – and there used to be certain small fields and knolls that were blue with harebells in late August – are becoming a furtive and fugitive species. There are fewer early-purple, and white, and pink-spotted orchids. The bog-asphodel thrives because it is poisonous, and the thistle because it is prickly; but most of the gentle and harmless are knuckling under. Swamp flowers such as kingcups and ragged-robin survive, and the annual field-gentian and centaury still carpet the clifftops; but the dark cities of the burdock are usually nibbled to ruins before they are completely built, and the wild angelica seldom grows tall, or erects its greenish-white umbrellas unmutilated. The wild carrot, which I suspect to be poisonous, usurps much of the machair that used to be a rich mixture of clovers, vetch, harebells and knapweed; and even the noxious ragwort never grows into fullsize plants, but flowers six inches from the ground.

The archetypal Scotch thistle is not really better off than it was under the dominion of man, because it really likes broken ground. These tall and magnificent biennials grow inside houses where the roofs have fallen, on the banks of streams or by the shore where there has been some erosion. The most successful thistle is a miserable, small-flowered, straggly runt that grows in great communal patches. And, of course, the nettle thrives.

For two or three years corncrakes called, like unanswered telephones, from the hearts of the dark nettle-forests; but these have now fallen silent and disappeared, probably prey to the interloping mink which multiply unchecked. Humans are at fault for introducing these versatile predators, and they are at fault in covering the land with sheep. Without the latter there would be more honeysuckle, more briar-rose thickets, more willow trees and more rowans. Certain round-leaved poplars would climb down from the inaccessible crags where they cling on for dear life, and a low forest of windbent trees would develop. But without man the weeds of cultivation would still be missing, as would the cultivated plants themselves. Oats, rye, barley and potatoes are also botany, and also beautiful. And one of the beautiful things about them is that they grow at the behest of people, beneath untameable crags and beside untrustworthy seas, enclosed in the bright geometry of fields.

St. Kilda

The great collector of Gaelic folk songs, Margaret Fay Shaw, who died in 2004 at the age of 101, visited this remote island community shortly before its evacuation in 1930. She provides one of the most beautiful, unsentimental and 'luminous' accounts ever written about this unique people.

A Courteous And Friendly People

Margaret Fay Shaw

As we neared St Kilda, the sea-birds were absolutely extraordinary. Of course it was late May when there was always a tremendous number of them coming to nest. When the siren blew, they rose up in clouds – fulmars and puffins, guillemots and gannets. Near the entrance of the long horseshoe bay of Hirta, the main island, the cloud lifted and gave that vision of wild beauty that has so often been described. The small islands looked inaccessible, but Hirta itself was a most pleasing place with good pasture on its giant velvet green slope reaching to the summit of Conachair, the highest sea cliff in Britain. In the strange northern light every stone on the hillside appeared almost luminous. There was a row of houses with chimneys smoking and people with many dogs were hurrying to the shore. A group put out to meet us in a heavy rowing boat. We had brought them sad news, for a young woman who had been taken off the island some months before had died in a Glasgow hospital. A trawler had taken a message from the islands that she had appendicitis and needed hospital treatment, but too long a time elapsed before she was collected from St Kilda and the treatment came too late.

We were told that we mustn't touch a dog, because they were mangey. Nor were we to eat anything of their food. The St Kildans had had a severe winter and were terribly short, though fresh supplies were on the ship. A big rowing boat came out full of people who boarded the *Hebrides* to get news, supplies, and to talk, and we then went ashore.

We were met by a most courteous and friendly people. Some of the women wore dresses of dark blue serge, with a very tight bodice and full skirt, sometimes with an apron. Their skirts were trimmed at the foot with a little strip of black velvet and they wore a little tartan kerchief or a little shawl – not a big shawl over the head, as they did in the islands. They had boxes of knitted socks and gloves to sell, blown sea birds' eggs and rolls of the St Kilda murrit tweed. The women were the spinners and the men the weavers. The wool was from the brown or murrit sheep on the neighbouring island of Soay. This peculiar breed must have been there when the Norsemen came more than a thousand years ago, for Soay means 'sheep island' in Old Norse and such a name would not have been given unless there was something unusual about the sheep. They are more like goats than sheep, and Peigi MacRae taught me a Gaelic song beginning:

> *The foot of the Hirta sheep,*
> *That was the nimble foot!*
> *That was the elegant sheep!*
> *The colour would grow on her back,*
> *She would need neither lichen nor soot,*
> *But spinning the wool to make trousers.*

The wool of these sheep is of a colour called 'moorit', that is, dark brown; they would not need to be dyed with lichen or soot. Their fleeces are not long and shaggy, but close and thick; they have to be plucked, not shorn with shears.

I made my way along the flagstone known as 'The Street'. The houses were broad and wide with tarred roofs – superior to many I knew in South Uist. Between them were the older dwellings, built of rough stones and used as byres. The church, with the schoolhouse, the manse, the nurse's house and the little wooden post-office were at the east end of the village, while behind the houses, scattered over the hillside were the countless 'cleits', small oval-shaped stone huts with flourishing green grass tops. In these storehouses were kept dried birds, meat and feathers. The sheep on Hirta were not the Soay breed but blackface; some had double horns and I was given a pair of these as a souvenir.

There was little chance to talk to anyone because of the sad news that we brought, and the meeting with the factor and the official was attended by all adult members of the community. However, I was invited by a Mrs Gillies to come in and sit by her fire. She was wearing a most becoming tartan square on her head. I thought she must have woven it herself, but when I admired it she asked: 'Do you know Cowcaddens? That's where it came from and I can give you a nice new one.' Her own had faded to such soft and pretty colours that I said I much preferred it. This made her laugh and she took it off and gave it to me, reluctantly taking half a crown. The scarf is still a prized possession.

My great ambition was to get up the side of the hill to get photographs. There was a passenger on the ship who said he would help me with my camera, so we started off. We were joined by a St Kildan lad, who showed us where they'd had a wireless station in the '14-'18 war. A German submarine had come and given them warning that they were all to hide because they were going to blow it up, which they did. It had never been mended and they'd had no communication since that time. And this boy said, 'You see, after all you couldn't blame them. They did what we would do.'

We got to the top of Conachair to look down from this tremendous cliff, and I got my photographs. It is down these cliffs that the St Kildans went on horsehair rope to gather sea-birds and their eggs. The guillemots' eggs the St Kildans sold were perfectly beautiful, a pale greeny blue, and covered with what looks like Chinese characters in black or dark brown. But I found that their colours would fade, even if you kept them in a box.

I didn't see any ponies at all, although there were cattle and plenty of sheep. There was no transport of any kind. The May light in the Hebrides lasts until midnight, but there on St Kilda, the steep cliff made a shadow by late afternoon and the whole island was dark green velvet. It was most eerie, this silence, as we made our way back to the village. Yet when I met the resident missionary, Mr Munro, and told him what a beautiful place I thought St Kilda was he replied, 'Yes, but it's the noise; I can't stand the noise.' Well, I couldn't think what noise at all, but I suppose he meant in the winter time – the winds and gales; then, it's a very wild place.

It was St Kilda's Queen's Nurse, Miss Barclay, who told us that the people were close to starvation. She had been there a couple of years and she told me that five of the men there had duodenal ulcers. There was hardly one able to do hard physical work, and they had got so listless that they didn't cut down into the peat; they just burnt the turf on the top. The cattle were so badly fed that the milk wasn't enough for the calves and themselves, so they killed the calves and fed them to the dogs. It was essential that the dogs survived because they were needed to catch and hold the sheep so that the wool could be plucked by hand. The St Kilda dogs were not like the collies I had seen in the Hebrides. They were smooth-coated and looked like old-type lurchers.

They had no sugar, no soda, and no potatoes. The nurse did have some jam, and the children came every day for a spoonful to give them some energy. The islanders had become such beggars that the trawlermen wouldn't give them anything. The deep sea trawlers would go in to shelter and if the St Kildans went out in their small boats to ask for food, they turned the hoses on them. Once they had asked the nurse to go out in the boat. She was absolutely terrified of the small boat but they were in such desperation, they pleaded with her to go. So she did go and stood up in the boat and called to them: 'Please give us some potatoes, because we have hardly anything to eat.' So they gave her some sacks of potatoes.

Charles MacLean writes of the rituals and beliefs surrounding the dead on this island where each death had a devastating effect on the community and was perceived as 'a victory for the other side'.

The Spirits Of The Dead
Charles MacLean

Deserted cemeteries often enjoy a longer half-life than the ruins of places where people have lived. The graveyard on Hirta still bears poignant witness to the departed community's lonely struggle for existence. Immured in a sad oval of stone, Cill-Chriosd, the Sepulchre of Christ, looks out across the roofless houses of the village to the bay beyond. An empty post and a red hinge are all that remain of the wooden gate which once kept out the islanders' cattle and sheep; lichen encrusts the random gravestones that emerge at unexpected angles from the overgrowth of rank vegetation; iris flags take light and shade from the wind as they bend where it blows. Despite the years of neglect and decay it is the only place on the island where the past keeps constant vigil over the present.

When there was a death in St Kilda the news was cried throughout the island so that everyone could stop work and return home. The relatives of the deceased at once began to howl and wail and to watch over the body for the next two or three days or as long as it was kept inside the house. Dirges were sung and laments composed, telling of the good deeds and fine character of the dead man, commending his soul. While the women watched and sang and wept, the men set about making a coffin with whatever wood was available. Others were kept busy catching sheep belonging to the dead man's family and baking bread. The amount of food prepared for the wake was proportionate to the honour to be paid to the deceased. It was an expensive custom for anyone who was unlucky enough to lose several relatives. When the grave had been dug and everything was ready, the funeral cortege set out for Cill-Chriosd. The coffin was carried on two poles by four young men who led the procession in the course of the sun's shadow, even if this meant trampling down crops, from the house to the graveyard. When they arrived at the cemetery they waited for the shadow of the sun to reach a certain position – adults were buried in the afternoon, children in the evening. Some prayers were said as the grave was filled in; then the mourners sat down on the grass and stones to eat their bread and mutton.

After the funeral the island went into mourning for a week, during which time little or no work could be done, the people being so overcome with grief and emotion. A death in St Kilda affected the whole community very deeply; everyone knew or was related to the dead person; and in a small isolated society every man, woman and child played an important part in the fight for survival. The loss of any human life was a victory for the other side and a harsh reminder to the community of its frailty.

In common with other Celtic peoples the St Kildans retained close contact with the spirits of the dead. The departed were never allowed to depart altogether, only to change residence. Souls inhabited rocks, streams, flowers, birds, animals, the bottom of a well, the edge of a cliff, almost anywhere, doing penance until released by prayer.

These transmigrations inevitably inclined the islanders to be superstitious. If one believed that every natural object harboured a soul in torment it was difficult to be otherwise. But their beliefs and superstitions were founded in the reality of a practical relationship with nature, in the islanders' everyday dependence on its bounty and their perpetual fear of its vengeance.

The St Kildans observed natural signs. They told the time of day from the course of the sun, not through the sky but over the land, noting when it struck certain rocks and parts of the hills. When there was no sun they watched the tides. They made weather forecasts, based on careful observation of sea, sky and the behaviour of the birds. But their applied study of nature was pervaded by superstition and the elaborate signs for telling some fantasy in the future were as meaningful to them as the more mundane indications of an approaching storm.

Lewis

One of the finest Hebridean poets, Iain Crichton Smith writes of the island where he grew up in the 30s and 40s: which he loves 'for its very bleakness, for its very absences'.

Moments Of Illumination
Iain Crichton Smith

Lewis was of course a bare island without a theatre, ballet, museums. There was a good library, however, and there I would sit during the dinner hour reading magazines like The Tatler bound in leather covers and seeing pictures of the aristocracy joined together by a "common joke." I got so engrossed in the magazine that I forgot to return to school until three o'clock and was saved from punishment by a very understanding lady teacher. I think that I liked the Nicolson very much. I became reasonably good at passing examinations. I even tried the Aberdeen University Bursary Competition in fifth year and won a minor bursary, although I had great difficulty with the Latin paper since all the "u"s had been printed as "v"s and at first I wondered whether I had been given a Hindustani paper.

I moved between two worlds – the world of school and the world of the village – travelling home every night by bus. I spoke Gaelic at home and English in the school. But in those days I did not find this an extraordinary situation: I simply accepted it. I would never have dreamed of speaking English to anyone in the village, and of course most of the Stornoway people spoke only English. I was not writing much Gaelic then, only English, and what I most wrote was poems. There were no interesting Gaelic books for me to read, no adventure stories, no poetry that spoke directly to me in my own world. I used to read Penguin New Writing – though cannot now remember where I got copies of the magazine – and learned about Auden and other writers who excited me very much.

I became, I think, slightly blasé in an objectionable and rather juvenile way. I began to think of the island as constricting. I could not but see that religion was dominant and joyless, that ministers were considered as of the greatest importance, that certain people whom I despised were respected simply because they were church-goers and attended the Communions. It was as if I was searching for a wider world of ideas which I could get only through books, a freedom which I imagined as existing elsewhere. I felt myself as alienated from my own friends for I had the feeling that I was predestined to be a writer – a poet certainly – though I had not written anything that was of the slightest value. I even felt that Stornoway, which had once seemed a pulsing city, was becoming smaller and duller. I thought of the black-clad women gossiping at corners, in the biting wind, while at the same time clutching their Bibles with black elastic around them.

I would return at night from the school and do my homework – I remember mainly geometry problems and Latin – by the light of the Tilley lamp on the oil-clothed table, and I felt more and more a gap opening between me on the one side and my mother and brother on the other. So I withdrew into myself and never discussed anything that had happened in the school as if it were a secret world which I treasured and which I did not want tampered with at any cost. I did not want to have anything to do with the cutting of peats, mainly because I was clumsy, and also because I felt that such tasks were unimportant: what was important was the world of the mind. I was continually falling in love with girls who I thought were at least as beautiful as Helen, but I never told them my passion. I only dreamed about them.

The only contact I had with the boys of the village was through football, for I played outside right for the village team. I was not particularly good but I valued the games partly for their own sake but also because by means of them I felt myself part of a team, of the village itself. Sometimes if I played well I thought there was nothing in the whole world like racing down the wing with the ball at my feet, the green dewy grass below me, and the possibility of a goal ahead of me. I would listen to the radio and almost cry with frustration when in every game Scotland was hammered by a forward line composed of people like Matthews,

Carter, Lawton and Finney. I could not understand why the English could keep their forward line intact throughout the whole war and thought that there must be a secret plot to keep these great and hated players available for the simple purpose of humiliating Scotland.

I had no feeling for Scotland at all as a country except through football. I did not feel myself as belonging to Scotland. I felt myself as belonging to Lewis. I had never even seen a train. I had never been out of the island in my whole life. Glasgow was as distant to me as the moon. I had hardly read any Scottish writers, not even MacDiarmid. Most of the writers I had read were English. The island was in a way self-sufficient and, strange though it seems, there were many parts of the island itself that I had never visited. For instance it was not until recently that I visited the district of Ness which is one of the most beautiful areas in Lewis. I travelled the beaten track between my village and Stornoway and it never occurred to me to go anywhere else, for hardly anyone had a car then, and we certainly did not have one. We were too poor. My mother and the three of us existed on a widow's pension of about a pound a week and most of this was spent on food. My books I got from the library or from friends, one in particular who lent me detective stories which he could afford to buy.

In a strange sort of way, too, the island seemed to have no history. There were standing stones on the moor behind our house but I never found out why they were there or who had put them there. My curiosity about the past was minimal and it never occurred to anyone to tell us anything about the history of the island. It seemed to have sprung out of the sea fully formed, scoured by the wind, brilliant in spring, with daffodils, without much animal life, and with few birds. It was a hard bleak island which did not reverberate when one touched it with one's mind.

Looking back on it now I think of its society as a very demanding one, classless, practical, and in some ways claustrophobic. One was judged by what one could do, not by one's money (for in those days very few people had much of that). The most important thing was to be practical, and I wasn't that. I have seen men from the village building their own house, which seems to me an astonishing achievement. They fished competently and did all sorts of jobs that I wished to do but could not: repairing fences, tarring roofs, cutting peats and so on.

I felt myself a dreamer in this practical world, naked and visible to it: and yet it was also a world that valued education, not just because education led to a valuable job but for its own sake too. Nevertheless, I sometimes have a nightmare in which I think that there are more teachers in Scotland than there are pupils, and I yearn for the love of ideas for their own sake: for the free play of the mind.

One of the most deeply perceptive and lyrical books written about Lewis in the 20th century is by the Australian, Rosemary Millington and here she describes the unearthly beauty of the Gaelic psalms sung in this spiritual home of the Free Presbyterian Church.

Voices From Every Heart
Rosemary Millington

Once inside I could still hear the booming of the ocean above the buffeting of the gale against the thin windows. The children had been pushed into a run all the way from home and they sat breathless between their parents, waiting for the service to begin. The missionary, if he was present, was invisible, folded deeply in his greatcoat and bent in meditation behind his solid lectern. At any moment he would suddenly rear up and fix his glasses on his congregation. He was thinking. What was he thinking – was he going over the salient points of his sermon, was he peering inconspicuously under the fringes of the lectern to see who was there, was he at prayer or wishing himself into a pious rate of respiration before summoning the Lord? It was like waiting for a séance to begin. I wished he would stand up and say, 'You go; find out the truth, I don't know any more than you do.' If he knew, the missionary would say that Satan was amongst us, the very devil.

When the time came the doors were closed, latecomers would have to return home.

The missionary rose unexpectedly from his crouching stomach-ache position; he appeared as black as penitence, large and tall in his dark overcoat. It seemed as if he had no eyes, just big round empty glasses that stared blankly in the dull light as he moved his heavy head to scrutinise us. The men winced and the women bowed their heads, specially the olden ones, and slapped their children's searching fingers away from pockets where sweets were waiting for distribution at the sermon. His eye fixed on me for a moment. It was as if he had never seen me before and did not know me. But he did. I looked straight back at him.

This was his day. The minister only came once every second Sunday of the month. The minister, now, he was a fine man, a fine figure of a man in every way, and everyone looked forward to his visits. He never lacked a dinner either for the women waiting behind after worship to invite him home – and already prepared for him whether he went or not. This was the missionary's day.

He gripped the edge of the lectern with both hands till the bones looked like claws and he raised both elbows like an eagle about to take off in majestic but wrathful flight, and with a deep breath he launched into the announcement of the first Psalm, remembering to repeat it in English for me, mildly. The precentor stood up and intoned up and down the first line of praise. Exultation! No one was shy to sing to his God. I heard the music on this Sunday that I had never heard before, except in my dream. As exuberantly as bugles the voices came from every heart, some stridently unblending with voices accustomed to singing above the wind on the moor and ocean.

I couldn't sing; I could only listen. I looked about, up at the tent-pitched roof with the bare beams, down the wooden whitewashed walls to the empty side where there was not a single body in any of the slightly crooked pews. Our side, the pews were squashed fully with a family to each; small and brawny men and broad women of all ages, and their littlies squeezed in between, fidgeting for a breath of air among the Sunday clothes and the strong emanations of sheep. The Sunday-special clothes hung all week beside the working togs well soaked in daily dealings with flocks on the grazings and chores on the croft. These suddenly reverent people were as vulnerable as hermit crabs out of a shell on a Sunday under the eagle eye of the missionary.

The Prayer. Not the Lord's prayer but a prayer of supplication and request even so. The service was almost like not going to church at all. Worship was from the imagination, invisible, there were no aids to the realisation of God except in the words of the missionary. It was like a child's prayer at night: 'God bless all of us.' The missionary prayed for everybody with his eyes shut because, O Lord, thy children met in this place, they did not want Hell Fire and Eternal Damnation. We were standing as upright as possible in the narrow pews, thinking severely of the task of addressing ourselves to the Lord. If we could not see Him in our mind's eye we lacked imagination.

North Rona

The poet, Kathleen Jamie spends a few days on this remote island in the north Atlantic, named after St. Ronan who built a chapel and an oratory. The island which was abandoned some 150 years ago was home to generations who lived and died 'all in the compass of this little island, always with the sound of the sea, far from anywhere else'.

From The Colours Of The Sky

Kathleen Jamie

The idea that remote islands are somehow "timeless" is a nonsense. Of course you want to slow down and fill your mind with space and sea, to examine every inlet and flower, but unless you want to be marooned, you always have to bargain with the weather. There are no safe anchorages on Rona, and Bob was concerned about the east wind. If it rose a couple of notches, as was forecast, we'd have to turn and leave again, simple as that. But we'd have the night at least, and probably the next morning, too. We went ashore in the tender, each choosing our moment to jump as it leapt in the swell, then clambered up slippery rocks on to the hillside. Just that small elevation, a hundred feet or so, gave an astonishing view: a green morsel of an island, already dipping back towards the sea, and the sea shifting away forever.

The seal researchers' bothy stands proud on the island's south side, like a garden shed pretending to be a lighthouse. A vague path led uphill towards it. A bonxie flew alarmingly close overhead, big and brown, but it didn't attack. Always there was the sound of surf, beating on the rocks.

There was a plan: after we'd pitched tents and had explored a while, we'd eat aboard the boat, then just as it was getting dark, we'd assemble in the derelict village. The day was long: it was almost 11 before the light drained from the sky. The village is encircled by fields that are still clearly defined on the ground. They're not square fields, but the old so-called "lazy-beds" – long, heaped-up mounds which alternate with drainage ditches. They rise and fall in waves, as though the land, being so close to the ocean, had assumed the same sea-swell. A narrow path winds through the lazy-beds to the abandoned village houses. Only when you're among the walls do you realise that's what they are: rough stone walls of dwellings, built half into the ground.

As night fell, the breeze grew colder. Darkness pooled in the ditches and the roofless shells of houses. Though the sky was clouded, a pewtery light lingered on the sea. We were gathered in the ruins for a purpose: one of our party, John Love, had established himself in the lee of a wall and set out a few tools: minuscule pliers, a small ruler and a spring balance. As night came on, quietly we listened to the surf and to the seals crooning mournfully from their rocks. Far over the sea, a full moon was rising, brightening the bank of cloud that was waiting to receive it. A solemnity fell over everyone, as we waited for things to begin.

Then, when it was quite dark, someone started chortling. Not a person, but a pixie. John and the other birders smiled and roused themselves. Again, and more: from gaps in the old walls came wonderful sounds of pixies and elves, burbling, chattering and riding little two-stroke scooters. The village walls, which we in our dull anthropocentric way call "poignant" and "silent", were alive with gleeful, tin-toy, chatterbox sounds; and then something flew quick and bat-like through the dark.

This is one reason ornithologists come to Rona. Leach's petrels are rare birds that live out at sea, and which come ashore only to breed. They nest in burrows, usually on clifftops, and come and go by night. To catch and ring them requires a special licence, which Love holds. He had spent the early evening erecting two mist-nets (a bit like badminton nets) across gaps between walls. Now the birds were plopping in like shuttlecocks.

It does them no harm. They didn't flutter, they just waited for deft hands to disentangle them. After it had been taken from the net, each bird was put in a cotton shoe-bag, and the bag carried to Love. We who'd never seen petrels before crowded for a look as he removed the first one. About the size of a thrush, but smoky dark, they have a tube nose like a fulmar's, and exquisite, tiny, black webbed feet. (The name petrel comes from Peter, who walked on water.) Love showed us the forked tail – the bird's full name is Leach's fork-tailed petrel – and demonstrated how best to hold the bird so it feels secure: you enfold it in your hand so its head sticks out between your middle and index finger. The fine feathers on the petrels' heads reminded me of the inside of puffballs: a rich, musty, dusty brown, but with a quick dark eye.

Love measured the length of each bird's wing, then he took a minuscule ring and, with the pliers, closed the ring around the bird's leg. Each ring is numbered, and for a while my small task was to act as scribe, noting by torchlight the number of the ring as he read it out, and the weight and size of the bird to which it was being attached. Before the birds were released they were weighed. Then, if you catch an individual again in the future, you'll know how old it might be, how well it's faring, if there are fewer or more than there were 10, 20, 50 years ago. Many of the night's birds were "re-traps". Though small, they can live for more than 30 years. How to weigh a petrel? You slip it back into its cotton bag, then hang the bag from your spring balance, being mindful to deduct the two grams the bag weighs: 48, 47, 50 grams, a scant two ounces of feather and bone – yet petrels winter far out at sea, weathering the storms. Then they're released, with a casual throwaway gesture that gets them airborne and away, none the worse.

By about 1a.m., after the chill hours lying queasily on the boat's deck, I was bitterly cold, and though the petrel party would go on till dawn, I was ready to retreat to my tent. Perhaps it was the effect of the cloud-obscured moon, but the island was gilded in a strange bronze light. It had been my birthday, and I'd been heaped with gifts: sea, and orcas, Leach's petrels and seals singing their loopy, consoling songs. As I climbed, fully clothed, into my sleeping bag, I noticed that my hands smelled. It was a funky smell, almost sexual, dusty and oily at once, the smell of petrels, like a mushroom made of whale breath and herring-scale.

Were it not for that lingering smell, I might have thought the petrel business a dream. The morning sunshine was bright, full of sea light. There, again, was the vastness of the sea. The wind was holding off, but clouds were building. We had breakfast on the boat, then went ashore again. I made my way across the hill and through the lazy-beds to the village and St Ronan's chapel, so to see them by daylight. The nets, of course, were gone. Love and the others had stayed till about 4am, and caught 100 birds. Now the low walls, and their coats of turf and lichen and tufts of sheep's wool, were again inscrutable.

The doorway to the chapel is so low you must creep through bent double. Within is a small rectangular nave. There is no roof now, only the dry-stone walls remain, but even with the sky above there is a feeling of age and sanctity. Great age: it's 1,200 years since St Ronan arrived in his boat. Leaning against the walls are some broken quernstones and a number of rough stone crosses, stained with bird droppings. Twin symbols of Rona life, you can sense toil in the quernstones, a residual paganism in the crosses.

In the chapel's eastern wall, a further low doorway opens in to the tall corbelled chamber of the saint's oratory. The lintel is hewn from quartz; the whole structure feels Neolithic. Inside, but for a small square window, the sea and sky are quite abolished. It smells of earth. A visitor from the inconceivable future, I remained for a short while, imagining what it was to sail the seas in a small boat until one found a faraway island, under a vast sky, where one could build a stone cell in which to pray. Could Ronan, at his most solitary and contemplative, have imagined these times to come? Easier to imagine the kingdom of heaven.

Pixies on motor-scooters, saints in their open boats, shipwreck and quernstones; it was true, I suppose, what someone whispered last night, as we stood in the darkened village waiting for the petrels: "Oh, you can feel your imagination run riot!" Now, in the light of day, I wasn't sure. Imagination, certainly, but not "riot". I crept out from the chapel into the bright day, and spent a little time in the graveyard where more crosses are slowly sinking into the soft earth. To be born and live and die, all in the compass of this little island, always with the sound of the sea, far from anywhere else, what would that do to your imagination? Martin Martin, the 17th century Gaelic travel writer from whom we glean so much, records one beguiling detail about the Rona people: "They took their surnames from the colours of the sky, rainbow and clouds."

Not riot, because I think places like Rona offer very clear direction to the imagination. The ancient chapel, the village and the long forsaken lazy-beds are truly poignant, truly evocative of a lost past. We can imagine that past as sweet, as though bathed in bronze light. As I crept around the houses, though, I wondered if such places aren't now offering us pictures of a possible future, too. A remote, changed future, when more once-inhabited places will be abandoned. We can see beginning already, flood here, drought there. We may need such images as Rona provides to help us imagine the world to come, because beneath the surf and birds' calls you can hear the long withdrawing roar of human occupation.

Inevitably, the chapel is in need of attention. The south-west corner is badly slewed out of true. The east wall was repaired last century, now the west needs work. The chapel, indeed the whole village, is a scheduled ancient monument. Ironic, in a way, that we've assumed a duty to preserve such places. It's illegal to tamper with them. It's illegal to cause change in these changed places, places that could offer us ways of thinking about change to come.

"Change" is a word you hear all the time from the ornithologists. The petrel-ringing was fun, and faintly ludicrous, but that's how you know when things are in need of repair, when things are slewing out of true. Down on the shore I could see the tall figure of Sarah Wanless, an expert sea-bird ecologist, moving around the rocks. There had been shags standing there, wings outstretched in their sepulchral way, and now she was looking for shag pellets. Shags, like owls, bring up what they can't digest, and from their pellets ("like a mixture of earwax and phlegm") Wanless can tell the species and age of the fish they've been eating. It all adds to the picture, increasingly grim, of what's happening in the north Atlantic. Already the birders had made a quick assessment of the numbers of breeding birds on the cliffs, the numbers of eggs they could glimpse at the guillemots' feet, and they were fearful that this year will be another famine year. A collision of over-fishing and climate change has left no sand eels for the puffin and guillemot chicks to eat. Adults are failing to nest, puffin chicks are starving in their burrows. Like MacLeod of old, the naturalists are returning from the Atlantic islands with doleful news.

Hoy

Mike Seabrook describes how one of Britain's most distinguished composers, Peter Maxwell Davies came to inhabit an abandoned croft house on this island of precipitous cliffs and ferocious winds.

The Lonely Cries Of Birds

Mike Seabrook

By this time – mid 1972 – Max had already started discussions with his friends in the Orkneys about the possibilities of restoring Bunertoon, the little croft that he had glimpsed in the rain during his first visit to Hoy. Then it had been a roofless ruin, open to anything the elements chose to hurl at it – 'just walls, with sheepshit up to here', Max described it, extending his arm at shoulder-height – but it was wonderfully situated, looking out over the boiling cauldron of the Pentland Firth. Max could see both its potential as just the lonely, utterly off-the-beaten-track hideaway he was seeking as a place in which to compose, and its actual virtues: it might be in a ruined condition, but what remained of it was built in the manner of Hoy: three feet thick and solid – very necessary to keep out the ferocious winds coming off the Atlantic.

At that time the ruin, although it was on land farmed by Jack Rendall, was owned by the Laird, one Malcolm Stewart, an absentee landlord who could not really afford to maintain the buildings on his substantial estates. Shortly afterwards he made it over to the Hoy Trust, of which a number of local dignitaries, including some of Max's friends, were members. In 1976, however, Parliament passed the Crofting Act, which enabled sitting-tenant farmers in Jack Rendall's position to purchase the land they farmed and any buildings that happened to be on the land. Bunertoon was among the properties bought from the Hoy Trust by Jack Rendall. By the time the Act was passed Max had already taken advice, decided that Bunertoon was potentially renovatable and habitable, and taken out a lease on it. With the passing of the Act, he simply stopped paying his rent to the Hoy Trust and paid it directly to Jack Rendall instead – and continued to do so until a very satisfying day in July 1985, when he bought it outright for £2,500. From the moment when he had first expressed an interest in coming to live in Rackwick, Jack had, of course, been quietly giving Max the once-over on behalf of the rest of the very close, tight-knit little island community, where a newcomer who did not fit in, especially if he was an arriviste from the mainland or, even worse, England, would be a potentially explosive nuisance. The fact that Jack sold Max the croft readily and without a moment's hesitation indicates clearly that Max had passed the test.

All the same, the renovation took over two years to complete. Archie Bevan's two sons, then aged about fifteen and thirteen, did the really strenuous part, shovelling out the huge quantities of droppings left inside by sheep taking temporary refuge over many years in the standing walls from the colossal winds off the Pentland Firth. Then Max called in a friend from England, David Nelson, and between them they began to turn the ruin into a habitable cottage. Nelson did the difficult parts such as the woodwork; as Max wryly puts it, 'I was relegated to jobs like pointing walls.'

The work proceeded slowly but steadily. A new roof was put on – after Max's ancient gramophone had been lowered in through the hole where the roof was to go: the horn was so enormous that there was no other way of getting it into the building. Eventually the little house was complete, and ready for human occupation for the first time in many decades. Max moved in in 1974, and was delighted with his new home from the first day. It was always comfortable enough, though in the early years he had no electricity there. Instead he would compose by the light of oil lamps, and keep himself and the cottage warm with an open fire, on which he burned driftwood, gathered in huge quantities off the beach in the nearest cove, and coal, which he lugged up to the cliff-top from the nearest point of delivery – Jack's farm, a mile away.

Since then he has had electricity installed (in 1980), and the little home now boasts a CD player, an iron stove to replace the open fire, and storage heaters to back it up. The lavatory, which in the early days had been a chemical affair, now has a proper soakaway, and there is an electric shower unit as well, both of them in a shed, as stoutly built as the croft itself, reached from the cottage door by a series of stepping stones leading through the garden, across a chattering little burn that bubbles and chuckles its way beside the croft and down the almost vertical cliff-face beyond. The only minor drawback with this arrangement is that the shed is roofed with a sheet of corrugated asbestos, and the corrugations make a perfect series of small entry points for the wind, which whistles eerily as it finds these entries and comes howling gleefully through them into the shed. Max's one concession to this is that in the winter he restricts his showering to once per two days, instead of once a day.

The most important thing about Bunertoon is that it provides what Max chose it for: peace, solitude and quiet. He does not get disturbed by holiday trippers; there are still very few air-force planes hurtling across the sky with their short-lived bolts of nerve-shattering sound; he looks out through his little window in its immensely thick embrasure, over his small plot of potatoes and a few other extra-hardy vegetables, then across a short sward of tough, curly, springy turf, and finally, over the lip of the steep cliff and straight out over the Pentland Firth. This ensures that although Max certainly has the quiet he needs, it is not silence. The Pentland Firth is one of the two roughest areas of sea in the world, alongside Cape Horn; a hundred feet or so below Max's cottage there thunders, all day and all night, all year round, a seething crucible of boiling sea, swept in by five tides and out by four more, churned and whipped by the vast winds of the region, and counterpointed by nothing except the lonely cries of birds. These are things that have become the very stuff of Max's music over the last couple of decades. To Max himself, they have become the daily stuff of life itself.

Orkney

Ronald Blythe visits one of the most distinguished island writers, George MacKay Brown in his small home which he rarely left. Shortly after this visit, George was to join 'the infinite dead of the island' he so much loved.

Interrogating The Silence
Ronald Blythe

The natives of extraordinary places show weariness at the visitor's reactions, so I try not to bore George with my sightseeing. Returning from the kirkyard I did have to ask him about the Scottish custom of Hellenic monuments rising from Presbyterian graves, the draped granite urn on its tall plinth being a favourite. At Stromness scores of them stretch from the grass as if to be visible from the sea. He hadn't noticed. It was what a traveller would notice and was useful. But he had noticed, needless to say. Nothing had escaped him. In *Five Green Waves* there is a perfect account of the scene I had just left:

'I wandered away from him among the branching avenues of tomb-stones – the tall urns and frozen angels of modern times; the fiery pillars with the names of grandfathers on them; the scythe-and-hourglass slates of the eighteenth century; the lichened leprous tombs of a still earlier age. This small field was honeycombed with the dead of generations – farm-ers with stony faces; young girls rose-cheeked with consumption; infants who had sighed once or twice and turned back to the darkness; stern Greek-loving ministers; spinsters with nipped breasts and pursed mouths. I stood on the path, terrified for a moment at the starkness and universal-ity of shrouds; at the infinite dead of the island, their heads pointing west-wards in a dense shoal, adrift on the slow tide that sets towards eternity'

George takes the opportunity to talk shop. Do I have an agent? No, he does not have an agent. Reviewing. 'They (The Glasgow Herald) send me something now and then.' He makes the fire up, makes another pot of tea, asks for news, saying, 'I put something down every day, although it may not be much. Do you do that?' My head is drumming with marvels, but am reserved about my walk to Maes Howe in its flowery meadow off the Stromness-Finstown road. A party of 'Jerusalem-farers,' or young Norse-crusaders, had taken shelter from bad weather in this superb Neolithic rites of passage room, in which every stone exactly fits, and they scribbled on its walls such things as 'Many a proud woman has had to enter here stooping.' The caretaker from the neighbouring cottage had made me go first. Another rune says – George's translation – 'Ingibiorg is the loveliest of the girls.' This room was already three and a half thousand years old when the Jerusalem farers sheltered here in 1151 and scribbled in their feathery hand. Nothing totally disappears in Orkney and the line between pre-history and written history is a faint one. From Ingibiorg's boys to the circle of the sun, or the Ring of Brogar. Calm planks of split flagstones, their tops shaped like scimitars, and their subsidiary circle the Stones of Stenness stand by two glittering lochs. Flotillas of swans pass below a monolith called the Watch Stone. The banks of the lochs are covered with what looks like sheet-celandine, so dense are the burnished heads. All around lie the long-dead. The four archaeologists are very much alive and are only about a foot down. There is a hand-carved stone ditch. Twenty-seven of the original stones are erect and one is covered with Victorian graffiti by the men with Orkney place-names. *Always by the shore*, wrote George,

> *Kirk and kirkyard*
> *Legends of men, their carved names*
> *Faced east, into first light, among sea sounds.*

Hugo brought him to Oxford to convalesce after the operation. For George, it must have been like getting better on the moon. His final Under Brinkie's Brae column in the Orcadian on 3 April 1996 warned,

'There is a price to be paid for Progress; already the 'tabs' are being shown us, one after another.'

His Requiem Mass was sung thirteen days later in St Magnus's Cathedral, on the feast day of the saint. His last written words were in praise of April, 'the month that tastes of childhood.'

Stones Like Jewels

George MacKay Brown

Children came at fairly regular intervals – my sister Ruby in 1911, Hugh in 1913, John in 1915, a brother Harold who died in infancy in 1917, Richard (Norrie) in 1919, and myself in 1921.

Early years are remembered in gleams only, and the gleams illumine what seem to be quite unimportant incidents. I remember sitting up in my pram, aged maybe two or three, and watching the silhouette of my father, in his postman's hat, against the window; he seemed to be reading a sheet of paper. But why that simple image remains, while thousands of other images lie buried forever in the unconscious, is a mystery.

Another early memory is of sitting on the doorstep when a tinker woman came to the door selling pins and haberdashery. As a child I was so upset by people and events that were not part of the everyday life of Stromness, that I fainted where I sat. A dream remains from childhood: I am sitting in a tinkers' pony-drawn cart, and we are going on a country road. I have never had a dream so vivid. They are taking me far away, up and down little hills.

Another memory is of the crew of an Aberdeen trawler; they are all drunk and staggering on the street. Whether I really saw this, or whether some neighbour woman told it at our open door, I can't now remember; but the image of those dangerous strangers on our quiet street filled me with dread.

A few years later, on a New Year's Day, I saw two of our local fishermen staggering on the street. They were both of them peaceable familiar men; the sight of them behaving in this bizarre way sent me hurrying home, white in the face. Later, one of my mother's friends said, 'May the fear of drink stay with him for a long time.'

I mention those trivial events because later, when I first began to write, tinkers and drinkers entered frequently into my stories and poems – too frequently, for many readers.

One reason, I think, is that such people are possessed of a wild precarious freedom denied to most people who are on the diurnal treadmill of money-making and accepted behaviour and whose days are folded greyly together. Actually, I have learned that this is not so; the life of everyone is unique and mysterious. Under all the accumulations of custom, boredom and drift lies somewhere 'the immortal diamond' spoken of by Gerard Manley Hopkins. Edwin Muir would have called it the 'Eden', a pure racial inheritance going right back to the Creation. I have often been intrigued by a latent snobbery that very many people, even the poorest and wretchedest, keep hidden somewhere about them; at the faintest encouragement they will tell you, in a secret proud whisper, how in fact they are not what they seem, they stem from an ancient proud lineage, they are connected with some duke a couple of centuries back, or going further into the mists, with a famous Viking jarl. I have wondered at the comfort such memories, of very doubtful validity, bring to ordinary people. It may be a spoiled fragment of the Eden that is such a wonderful symbol in Muir's poetry, or a distorted whisper of the intimations of immortality that Wordsworth had. I wonder at this preoccupation with the broken fragments of lost kingdoms myself – this gazing into stones as if they were jewels – because I have never had the least desire to know for sure that I'm descended from an earl or a great hero. I remember whispers in our house, in childhood, that somehow we could trace a descent from King Hakon, the tragic hero of Largs; but that must have been childish romancings of my sister and brothers. My father would have stamped sternly on such idle dreams: kings and millionaires meant nothing to him – his heart was always with the very poor and the dispossessed.

Twentieth-century literature has taken up the theme of the ordinary ineffectual man: Joyce's Leopold Bloom, Eliot's Prufrock, Beckett's Estragon and Vladirmir, Mann's Hans Castorp, Chekhov's drifters and dreamers on the edge of social catastrophe. It is remarkable that in modern literature it is the common man who holds the rarest treasures. There, lost, is the 'immortal diamond'.

Wyre

Edwin Muir vividly recalls the intense experiences of his childhood when he confronted beauty, violence and death, living on a tiny island where every aspect of human experience is brought near and is, therefore, inescapable.

The Original Vision
Edwin Muir

When I think of our winters at the Bu they turn into one long winter evening round the stove – it was a black iron stove with scroll work on the sides, standing well out into the kitchen – playing draughts, or listening to the fiddle or the melodeon, or sitting still while my father told of his witches and fairicks. The winter gathered us into one room as it gathered the cattle into the stable and the byre; the sky came closer; the lamps were lit at three or four in the afternoon, and then the great evening lay before us like a world: an evening filled with talk, stories, games, music, and lamplight.

The passing from this solid winter world into spring was wild, and it took place on the day when the cattle were unchained from their stalls in the six months' darkness of the byre, and my father or Sutherland flung open the byre door and leaped aside. The cattle shot through the opening, blind after half a year's night, maddened by the spring air and the sunshine, and did not stop until they were brought up by the stone dyke at the other end of the field. If anyone had come in their way they would have trampled over him without seeing him. Our dog Prince, who kept a strict watch over them during the summer, shrank before the sight. That was how spring began.

There were other things connected with it, such as the lambing; I think our lambs must have been born late in the season. I have a picture of my mother taking me by the hand one green spring day and leading me to the yard at the back of the house to see two new-born lambs. Some bloody, wet, rag-like stuff was lying on the grass, and a little distance away the two lambs were sprawling with their spindly legs doubled up. Everything looked soft and new – the sky, the sea, the grass, the two lambs, which seemed to have been cast up without warning on the turf; their eyes still had a bruised look, and their hoofs were freshly lacquered. They paid no attention to me when I went up to pat them, but kept turning their heads with sudden gentle movements which belonged to some other place.

Another stage in the spring was the sowing. About that time of the year the world opened, the sky grew higher, the sea deeper, as the summer colours, blue and green and purple, woke in it. The black fields glistened, and a row of meal-coloured sacks, bursting full like the haunches of plough-horses, ran down each one; two neat little lugs, like pricked ears, stuck up from each sack. They were opened; my father filled from the first of them a canvas tray strapped round his middle, and strode along the field casting the dusty grain on either side with regular sweeps, his hands opening and shutting. When the grain was finished he stopped at another sack and went on again. I would sit watching him, my eyes caught now and then by some ship passing so slowly against the black hills that it seemed to be stationary, though when my attention returned to it again I saw with wonder that it had moved. The sun shone, the black field glittered, my father strode on, his arms slowly swinging, the fan-shaped cast of grain gleamed as it fell and fell again; the row of meal-coloured sacks stood like squat monuments on the field. My father took a special delight in the sowing, and we all felt the first day was a special day. But spring was only a few vivid happenings, not a state, and before I knew it the motionless blue summer was there, in which nothing happened.

There are zones of childhood through which we pass, and we live in several of them before we reach our school age, at which a part of our childhood stops for good. I can distinguish several different kinds of memory during my first seven years. There is first my memory of lying watching the beam of light, which I associate with no period and when I still seemed to be in the cradle. After that come my memories of the baptism and the singing at the concert; these belong to my petticoat stage, when I was conscious of myself as a small child moving safely among enormous presences. Next – as if my mother's fitting me out with trousers had really changed me – I remember myself as a boy, aware that I was different from little girls; no longer in the world where there is no marriage or giving in marriage.

This stage seems to have coincided with an onset of pugnacity, for my first memory of it is a fight with another boy over a knife. The memory is dim, and the figures in it huge and shadowy, making me think of the figures in the Scottish ballads, the Douglases and Percys. It must have been in autumn, for a sad light hangs over it. The other boy, whose name was Freddie, was standing with me at a place where two narrow roads crossed, and a little distance away two older girls with cloths over their heads were watching. Dusk was falling; the wet clouds hung just over our heads, shutting us in and making a small circular stage for the combat. I remember my anger rising and lifting my hand to strike. I knocked Freddie down and snatched the knife from him. He did not get up again, that frightened me. I went over and shook him by the shoulder, and saw that he was crying as he lay with his face in the damp grass. A doctor had been to the house a little while before to attend to my mother, and I decided to be a doctor, went over to Freddie again, pretended to feel his pulse, and declared that he had recovered. How it ended and what became of the knife I do not remember.

This memory belongs to a different world from my other memories, perhaps because my pugnacious phase lasted only a short time, for after an attack of influenza I became timid and frightened. Other things as well may have helped to bring this about: I can give no clear explanation of it. In an island everything is near, for compressed within it are all the things which are spread out over a nation or a continent, and there is no way of getting away from them. A neighbouring farmer who had often brought me sweets in his snuff-lined pockets had died in great pain a little time before, and I had heard all about his death: I can still feel the terror of it. I have often fancied, too, that in a child's mind there is at moments a divination of a hidden tragedy taking place around him, that tragedy being the life which he will not live for some years still, though it is there, invisible to him, already. And a child has also a picture of human existence peculiar to himself, which he probably never remembers after he has lost it: the original vision of the world. I think of this picture or vision as that of a state in which the earth, the houses on the earth, and the life of every human being are related to the sky overarching them; as if the sky fitted the earth and the earth the sky. Certain dreams convince me that a child has this vision, in which there is a completer harmony of all things with each other than he will ever know again. There comes a moment (the moment at which childhood passes into boyhood or girlhood) when this image is broken and contradiction enters life. It is a phase of emotional and mental strain, and it brings with it a sense of guilt. All these things, the death of a man I knew, the sense of an unseen tragedy being played out around me, the destruction of my first image of the world, the attack of influenza, may have together brought about the change. In any case I became timid and frightened.

Papa Stronsay

Adam Nicholson movingly relates his encounter with the Transalpine Redemptorists monks who have built their Golgotha monastery on a small Orkney island. He finds that their deep attachment to tradition can have a strangely liberating effect.

Life From A Stone

Adam Nicholson

The next day was our last in Orkney. The weather was mild and sunny, with light southeasterlies forecast, a perfect and easy ride to the loneliest of all the Atlantic islands, three hundred miles north by north-west of us. We were going to the Faeroes. The long, easy lines and the pale, bleached colours of Orkney looked like a benediction. I had been deeply impressed by the twenty-five monks of the Golgotha monastery. Even that name is a signal of something. They came here in 1999, settling on their uninhabited speck of grass and rock because it represented 'a desert in the ocean', the sort of place monks have always sought out, away from the temptations and distractions of the city, to be named not after a version of Paradise or Eden but Golgotha, the place of the skull.

It is as profoundly conservative a regime as you can imagine. Every moment of the day, from its beginnings at three in the morning, when the island generator is turned on in preparation for the first mass at 3.45, to its conclusion in silence at seven in the evening, sleep at eight, is tightly and exactly regulated. There is no speaking at meals, nor in their prepara-tion or washing up. Dishes are cleaned to the singing of Latin hymns. The two novices among the twenty-five are allowed no jam with their bread and must remain in silence at all times. Every mass is said in Latin, since these monks are traditionalist Catholics, excommunicated by the Vatican, whose modern liberal drift they have rejected. This is a place devoted not to freedom but to obedience, the sanctity of tradition and the ancient Rule, even at the cost of broken relations with the Holy See.

The monastery is still raw in its newness: the chapel, for all its icons and the enrichments of its Catholic imagery, is in a converted herring gutting shed, the refectory in an old cow barn. The brothers' cells, in one of which I had been staying, are two long rows of small single-storey buildings, which are for the moment a stark and strange new addition to the Orkney landscape.

The abbot or vicar-general, a fifty-year-old New Zealander, Father Michael Mary, an amused, intelligent man, full of energetic visions for his future, told me, quite unequivocally and with a steady look straight into the back of my eyes, that as an agnostic, who didn't believe that Jesus was God, I was going to hell. I said I didn't believe in hell either. 'You might as well say,' he said touching the table between us, 'that this is made of marshmallow. It isn't. It's wood and you can't deny the realities.'

For all this exactness, this holding to many precise details of a long monastic tradition, in which there is nothing like television or radio, no private property, where all clothes and possessions (except toothbrushes and underwear) are shared, there is an astonishing absence of harshness. The discipline creates an air of ease and generosity. There is even, extraordinarily, a kind of gaiety about the monastery, laughter in the cowsheds as the monks milk their small herd of Jersey cows; as they build a new tractor house down by the pier, their habits smeared in mud and cement; as the little monastery launch makes its way to and from the pier on Stronsay; or as the two monks who are learning the bagpipes practise, the notes wobbling and wailing out on the edge of the old walled fields.

Perhaps this is obvious enough: the commitment to tradition, the deep engagement with the exactness of a monastic way of life, liberates these men in their daily dealings with the world and other people. Father Michael Mary said to me as we were walking to the monastery's own hermitage, away from the main buildings down on the shore, that 'you only have to pick up the tradition which is lying there beside you, unused on the ground, to find that it is living in your hand'. And that is exactly what it felt like: life from a stone. The *Auk* and the monastery, in other words, seemed to be opposed to each other: a desire for freedom against a desire for certainty; the rattled against the constructed cage; tension and distance against conviction and warmth.

Father Michael Mary and one of the monks, a smiling, red-bearded man, Brother Nicodemus, came to see George on the boat and he showed them everything for hours. When they had done, he asked them if they would come and bless the *Auk*. In the early afternoon, the community of monks arrived down on the quay. Father Michael Mary was dressed in the white alb and the scarlet and gold embroidered chasuble and stole of his office. George and I stood beside the monks as they gathered around us in their black habits. Will Anderson, Johann Perry, the cameraman, and Paul Paragon, the sound man, prepared to film, and the ceremony began. The men, led by Father Michael Mary, started to sing their Latin hymns to us and to the *Auk* as one of the brothers sprinkled holy water on her decks from a silver vessel, walking alongside her, sprinkling first at the stern, all through the cockpit, on to the side-decks, up by the mainmast, on to the foredeck and finally to her bow, while the seamless and beautiful hymns floated out over the boat, us, and the water. Phrases came drifting at me – 'Maria Stella Maris', 'Noah ambulante in diluvio', Jonah and Job, St Paul undergoing his great storm en route to Malta. Every person in the Christian tradition who had suffered at the hands of the sea, and was in need of protection from it, was summoned to our aid. All around us, their sonorous, unaccompanied, chanted voices swelled and encompassed us.

What is it about a blessing? The way it suddenly releases such a river of sadness? I felt an extraordinarily powerful grief rising up in me, waves of it, unexpected, unsummoned, unwanted. I looked across at George and saw him in a state of collapse, his face crumpled as if someone had punched him. My own tears came more as a kind of choking than anything else. I had to hold my face in my hands. I saw that Johann was crying. Why were we like this? It was not simply the beauty of the moment, although it was beautiful. Nor was it a matter of conversion or belief. None of us were 'getting God' that afternoon. In a way it was simpler than that. We were weeping, I think, because, for once in all our lives, a strong hand, the hand of tradition, embodied by these people we scarcely knew, believing things we did not believe, seemed to be coming up beneath us, broad enough to carry us, broad enough even to gather the battered, stalwart *Auk* in its folds, and, having taken us up like that, was now pouring a blessing over us. It was as if, in an act of powerful theatre, that tradition of strictness and self-abnegation to which these men had devoted their lives had become, for a moment, fatherly to us, in a way that, grown men as we were, ever required to be self-sufficient and upright in the world, we had not known for many years. It was, in other words, an act of sustaining love. Father Michael Mary gave me a rosary and Brother Nicodemus gave George the rosary from around his own neck. Neither of us could speak.

Papa Westray

Jim Hewitson warns those who dream of going to live on a small, remote island to escape from the pressures of urban living and to embrace 'the simple life' that they will be entering a community with its own complex set of rules and values.

Arcadia Among The Skerries

Jim Hewitson

Although visitors to Orkney may find the abandoned, desert islands with their roofless crofts, rusting farm equipment and tumbledown jetties atmospheric, I find them infinitely sad. The wind cries out for the generations who brought life to the hearth, the fields and the shore. These empty places are a sad legacy of communities and townships who failed to cope with the pressures of the twentieth century when the just expectations of young folk for a less severe lifestyle could often only be met across the water, as we've seen. As this century draws to a close two factors have combined to begin to turn this situation on its head. The first is tourism and the second, the influx of settlers from south – the not so quiet invasion.

Gone are the days on Papa Westray when horse and oxen teams worked every available field, the fleet of fishing skiffs went out in strength, when kelp was big business and babies were baptised with regularity. While farming in particular still holds sway, the tourist trade now touches most families on the island.

At this crossroads for the island several schools of thought meet. There are people on Papay who are convinced we should go flat out to exploit the boom while it lasts, others argue that with increased leisure time tourism is certain to grow steadily and look for phased development to protect our special social and physical environment and there are others who simply get on with the work around the farm and wonder what all the fuss is about. However, for such a small island the debate is significant. Learning from mistakes made elsewhere, it should be possible because of the convenience of scale to strike a balance between these two extremes, conservation and development.

The other intriguing element in this modern-day 'Orkneyinga Saga' is the arrival of the growing numbers of incomers, white settlers, ferry-loupers or just 'thae folk fae sooth'. Compromise will be necessary in this sector, too, if Orkney and its component islands are to benefit from this infusion of fresh blood and new ideas.

For a thousand years these islands have accepted settlers from far afield and the happy integration of the latest batch, as we approach the century's conclusion, is vital if Orkney is to flourish.

On this occasion the islands are being asked to absorb a very diverse bunch from an outside society where values are being transformed. They consist of the disenchanted, the disaffected, the neurotic, those who seek solitude or beauty, those who wish to work in a community where their role is immediately discernible and not lost in an urban scramble, those who seek to be part of a strictly defined society where they can bring up their children in a safer and cleaner environment, a few who will patron-isingly try to impose their theories of life on a sensitive and intelligent people, those who wish to be big fish in a small pond, clients of the DSS, those who can no longer cope with urban life and simple misfits like myself.

Blind animosity and whispered prejudice will, however, have to be put to one side if this partnership is to be achieved ... if Orkney is not to be split into two societies. An understanding of the ground rules which must apply in this coming together is essential.

New arrivals must prepare themselves psychologically for a lifestyle which, although less pressurised, remains complex, where tolerance and, above all, patience are essential. In Orkney, *mañana* is often even further off than in Latin lands. Being prepared for all eventualities (power cuts, cancelled ferries, etc.) and never expecting too much are also useful disci-plines. Your Sunday papers will never arrive on Sunday and if you need the dentist or the optician then it's a flight into Kirkwall. Unwritten rules include mucking in when required and being prepared to pass the time of day with the neighbours. The key for new arrivals is to follow these traditions. Start trying to change them and you might as well start looking for a new home.

But this is not one-way traffic. Islanders must exhibit understanding. Many still find it odd that people should tear themselves away from the relatively affluent south. People with influence in the community must take a lead in ensuring that if newcomers offer their talents openly and without precondition, seeking to serve rather than direct, then they must be made welcome. It must also be made certain that local people, particularly young adults, are not disadvantaged in the housing and jobs markets.

Islanders must guard against resentment and irrational hostility prompted by strange accents, attitudes and ideas and, while it's natural for remote and embattled communities to want to weigh up new arrivals, surely the incomers shouldn't have to plant three generations in the kirkyard before they're really 'at home'. For the small island communities there just isn't time left for such caution.

It's a humbling experience to stand on the rock shelves below St Boniface and scan the jumble of buildings and scattered masonry exposed in the bank by the summer dig. These stones, a procession of pasts, which stand witness to triumph and tragedy, joy and despair, are a poignant reminder of the remarkable continuity of human endeavour on this little dot of an island clinging to the Atlantic edge.

Maybe it takes a footloose pilgrim like myself, who pays social calls on sandstone slabs and who, through my own inadequacies, stands just a little apart from the action, to report on the important chapter currently being written in the annals of Papay. Are we building Arcadia among the holms and skerries of Orkney? Is Papa Westray's golden age just around the corner? Will it even be a good try or are we destined to be swept away beneath the flowing tides of social and physical change? Even in this land of elastic time I may not be around long enough to have these questions answered but the stones, unmoved by transient human ambition, will note the outcome. As ever.

Meanwhile the greatest expression of hope for this amazing place is contained in the final line of every exciting longrunning serial....
TO BE CONTINUED.

Papa Stour

The schoolteacher, Stella Shepherd memorably relates the steady erosion of a small island's population and the conflicting reactions of the few who remain to face the storms of winter.

Empty Pegs

Stella Shepherd

Although the island has an undoubted hold on its people, harsh necessity caused the drift away to continue. The numbers dwindled past the turn of the century, and have continued to decline up to the present day. The educational system does little to help the problem of depopulation, by making it necessary for older pupils to go to the town schools for secondary education. This is tantamount to drawing away the life-blood of the island and leaving it impoverished. My first personal experience of this came very soon after I arrived here.

Already one of my pupils was due to leave the Papa Stour school and to go to the mainland for further education. This was young George Sinclair. Coming as I did in May, it seemed no time at all after settling in that the summer exams would be set, the marks would be added up, the prize day arranged; then the term would be over. As far as my pupil, George, and I were concerned, it was hello and goodbye within a few short weeks.

We saw him off, and as the boat pulled away I wondered what the future would hold in store for him. How would he like the big world outside? And what choice of a career would be his?

When the next term started with a school roll of seven, I missed George, with his ready smile and his meticulous books. Yet his going was in the general order of things. To the children, it seemed natural enough. The empty desk was pushed into a corner, and life went on very much as before.

But when the next departure took place, a very different spirit prevailed. Edwin, George's younger brother, was the next to go. The whole family had decided to leave the isle, and when the harvest was gathered in from the rigs, and the year's work on the croft all completed, they packed and sailed away. I had promised the remaining schoolchildren that we would hoist a tablecloth upon a pole, and wave goodbye to Edwin, as the little craft crossed the Sound. It was a November day, and although the youngest waved their handkerchiefs, and one of the older boys held up the pole in salute to the departing boat, all the children seemed dispirited. When at last they turned back to the school, their sense of deflation was plainly to be seen, in slumped shoulder and listless eye. Perhaps Edwin's departure in the middle of the term had something to do with it, or the dullness of the heavy November day; but deep down, underlying these things, was the knowledge that a whole family, not just one boy, had left the isle.

Very soon after this, another departure took place, and this one had the most far-reaching effects of them all. It did not only affect the school. I lost another two pupils, my only girls, and was left with an all-boys' school. But the kirk lost an elder, and its congregation was further depleted; then the shop and post office not only changed hands, but changed premises too. All this happened when Alex, the shopman, and his family left the isle.

At their going, Lowery and his family departed too, and as Lowery had been the postman, someone else had to be found to deliver the mail. Then it was that Mary o' Biggins became our first post-lady.

For some time after these departures there was little change on the island. The school roll stood at four. The even tenor of life continued for some little while, until Willie o' Bragasetter decided to move, with his family, to the mainland. This did not affect the school, yet their going left not only an empty house, but a vacant spot in our day. We missed Willie's cheery wave and greeting as he passed the house on his way to the shop.

As one year succeeded another, the sad subtraction sum went on. Michael first, then John after him, sat the eleven-plus examination and subsequently left the island to go to Lerwick school. My school roll was now reduced to two – namely, Gordon and Billy, except for two short spells when Sandra attended the school temporarily. But, as time went on, I was very often teaching a single pupil, as Billy became seriously ill. But a worse blow was yet to fall.

One morning, towards the end of the arithmetic lesson, there was a knock upon the school door, and Mary stood there with the post. For her to come to the school door was a most unusual thing indeed. Her normal practice was to deliver the mail at the schoolhouse. There was something so downcast and sad about her mien as she bent to take the letters from the bag that I felt a sudden premonition. She murmured an apology for interrupting school, and when she looked up her eyes were brimming with tears, and her face red from weeping. Billy had died, she said.

It is difficult to express the rush of feelings that overwhelmed me; grief, shock, pity for his parents, sympathy for Mary, his aunt, and an infinite sadness. What I said, I do not remember, but when she had gone, I stood for one brief moment in the cloakroom thinking of the first thing, the immediate thing, to be done.

Gordon sat in the quiet schoolroom, alone; the door had been left open; so it was most likely he would have heard our voices and already have learnt the sad news. In any case, he would guess it from my face. In less time than it took to re-enter the schoolroom, what I must say had already formed in my mind, 'Except a grain of wheat fall into the ground and die, it abideth alone.'

Whalsay

Hugh MacDiarmid lived most of the 1930s in a small crofthouse called 'Sodom' where he wrote some of his finest poetry. He writes with deep appreciation of the island's crofters and fishermen who belonged 'to an age when man's sense of the drama of life was strong'.

Content To Be Human

Hugh Macdiarmid

I could not have lived anywhere else that is known to me these last four years without recourse to the poorhouse. We were not only penniless when we arrived in Whalsay – I was in exceedingly bad state, psychologically and physically. I am always least able to 'put my best foot forward' and do anything that brings in money when I am hardest up. I do my best work when I have most irons in the fire, and the fact that here I had all my time to myself and had 'nothing to do but write' for a long time made it almost impossible for me to do anything at all and is, recurrently, a drawback still. Besides, I was 'out of touch with things' – I had not the advantage of being 'on the spot' where 'anything might be going and worst of all I had no books. Indeed, we had practically no furniture. I succeeded in getting a nice commodious four-roomed cottage standing on a hillside and looking out over a tangled pattern of complicated tideways, *voes*, and islands with snaggled coasts to the North Shetland mainland and the Atlantic – for 27 shillings *per annum*! Houses are practically impossible to get; I got mine because a little earlier a child had died in it under tragic circumstances, and the islanders were fighting shy of it. I have forgotten what that first winter was like; no doubt my wife remembers all too well – it must have been one long nightmare of cold and damp and darkness and discomfort. Comfort never mattered very much to me, and after all one of my poems begins 'To Hell with Happiness', and I have always been accustomed to practice what I preach – I only write what I live. I am not a 'knacky' person; what furniture we had at the beginning was made for the most part by my wife out of orange boxes, tea boxes, and the like.

Somehow or other – in the face of all likelihood – we have flourished (never sufficiently, of course, to be secure at any time for more than a week ahead). Tonight as I sit writing, the cottage is amply and comfortably furnished, and though I have never succeeded in securing again many of the books which were the background of my own earliest books and which, many of them, were and remain so vital to my creative processes that in their absence I have subtly to reorient my writing in other directions than, if I could recover my old collections, I would be likely to take, many hundreds of books have accumulated about me again; all my principal intellectual interests are well represented and catered for – geology, biochemistry, plant ecology, physiology, psychology and philosophy – and I have a fine array of the works of my favourite writers, Rainer Maria Rilke, Charles Doughty, Stefan George, Paul Valery in poetry, Leo Chestov in philosophy, Pavlov's *Lectures on Conditional Reflexes*, and Lenin, Stalin, Marx, Engels, Adoratsky, and other dialectical materialist writers.

It is not a restful place in which to write. The cottage is rattling like a 'tin lizzie' in 90 miles-per-hour wind, and every now and again there is a terrific rattling of hail. We have had well-nigh continuous gales, with heavy snow – storms and great downpours of rain, for the last two months – the worst winter the Shetlands have had within living memory.

It is, indeed, a curious turn of fortune's wheel that has pent me in this little cottage where I who used to be so active in public work of all kinds a few years ago, and who 'went everywhere and knew everybody', can go for a week at a time and see no one to exchange a word with – nay, even so much as get a passing glimpse of anyone – except my wife and son; and, indeed, except for the local doctor (a friend whose presence here brought me to this island rather than to any of the sixty other inhabited islands in this archipelago) and one or two others, I go in this case often, not for a week, but for a month at a time.

*   *   *

How do I get on – in so far as I encounter them at all – with the local crofters and fishermen?

These men belong to an age when man's sense of the drama of life was strong and undimmed by the physical ease and psychological difficulty of urban living. It may be said of them, as Pierre van Paassen says of the people of Bourg-en-Forêt:

Those peasants amongst whom we lived were poor in worldly goods; they lacked many of the modern amenities of life, but they did not envy those who had them. Thoughts of tomorrow did not torture them. Their rule was 'to cultivate their own gardens'. I think that the serenity of their existence, which often evoked the envy of strangers who watched them, resided in the fact that they insisted on being men before social beings. They were individualists. They were content to be human. Thus they had retained something of that fundamental dignity which is the sole condition of human happiness because it is both our physiological norm and the law of nature.

Foula

The distinguished film director, Michael Powell recalls his unforgettable sixteen weeks on Britain's remotest inhabited island.

Where The Glittering Paths Meet

Michael Powell

I am the wrong person to write an appreciation of this book: my knowledge of Foula is so complete and yet so scanty; the sixteen weeks I spent there, struggling to make "The Edge of the World," were full of experience, but it was experience directed towards one end, to tell my story and to present to the world the most complete picture that I could of its background. Foula.

Two things came out of those weeks in 1936: our film, which, I think, will yet make Foula one of the best known places in the world, instead of the least; and the other is a love for the island and its people.

So perhaps I have a right to this page, after all.

An island has a personality of its own, the more remote, the more insistent. Why has an island an irresistible appeal to us all?

I think that the answer is because it is complete. We can see it as a whole. Other places have the same appeal, that we can feel at the first visit, but not in such an intimate, such a concentrated form. A lonely island throws its spell over the traveller as soon as he sets foot on its smallest rock.

So it was when I first saw Foula. On a still night in June we neared the little lights of Ham voe at midnight. We were six hours out from Scalloway in a motor-boat. The five peaks of the island lay black against a violet sky. A few fishermen were out under the cliffs. On the port bow the moon shone across the sea and on the starboard the setting sun was shining, and the two glittering paths met and broke in our wake. I have never forgotten it.

My film tells the tale of the defeat of a people. It was created and brought to life by the help of the people of Foula. They one and all proved more helpful, more sympathetic and more truly intelligent than any men and women with whom I have worked.

Whatever the critics say, the real star of my film is the lonely island of Foula – and the real makers are its people.

Sheila Gear writes of the simplistic and changing attitudes of mainlanders to Foula, whose residents have achieved a way of life too individual and subtle 'to conform to a uniform standard'.

Standing Alone
Sheila Gear

The attitude of others to our island has changed considerably over the last hundred years. Once it was considered just a piece of land the same as anywhere else and treated as such. People lived there in the same conditions as they lived in the rest of Shetland and indeed in most of rural Britain. They had their own particular traditions and ways of doing things but basically life was much the same. However improved communications brought Foula more to the eye of the public and it profited popular writers and the mass media to romanticize and dramatize the island. It became Britain's remotest island, the Edge of the World, the furthest outpost, cut off for months on end while the brave and noble natives starved – all calculated to appeal to the public's imagination and provide them with a few minutes of sensationalism. But the isle hadn't changed. It was still the same little piece of earth with folk going about their business as ever. Only now it could be officially declared "Out of this World". A very handy phrase for officials not wanting to provide it with the required amenities or even keep up the few it had. "Out of this world – you can't expect us to treat it like the rest of the country."

Although there is never any question of mass evacuation such as occurred in the case of St Kilda, it is unfortunately an inescapable fact that in the past its population, too, dwindled slowly away. We will live out our lives here, and our children too in their time, but what of their own children, what of the future? Will the island be empty after they are gone?

And we wonder if it will matter. But it does matter, it matters to us intensely. Why? Obviously there are personal reasons, we want to live out our lives here because we are happiest here and we hope our children will find the same contentment. As well as individual feelings, another important motive is survival of the tribe, a primitive instinct that has never been shaken off no matter how civilized man claims to be. There will always be "us" and "them" – Foula and the rest of the world. We may squabble over petty incidents, disagree over major issues, even dislike each other, but there is still a bond between us.

But does it matter to anyone else? Visitors sometimes ask what value this small isolated community can have to the rest of the world. It contributes so little to the country's economy and the people seem to have such a struggle to maintain their low standard of living. Would it not be better if they all left? Yet if they did there would be an immediate outcry. Why was this allowed to happen, they would ask, and learned books would be written to explain the reasons for the island's death.

I could warble on about the "way of life" and the importance of preserving it, the standard answer given by students of such things. Not that we don't have our way of life, but it isn't their concept of it. Our way of life isn't their happy illusion of a Utopian island of dreams where one has all the time in the world to stand and watch the hay grow. Nor is it the way of life imposed upon us by poverty and adverse conditions because we cannot do any better. The only folk wishing to preserve the spade instead of the plough are those who don't have to do any digging. Our way of life is more subtle – a harmony with our island, an understanding of it, an acceptance of the hard aspects as well as the good. With the increasing spread of urbanization this relationship with the land is disappearing, the city dweller no longer has the stimulus of man's natural environment, he has to invent his own artificial "island" to provide him with kicks, hence the appalling increase in materialism. Obviously this cannot be solved by everyone going "back to the land" for the population has become too large for this to ever be practical. But let those who have a real island to return to be encouraged to do so. It is possible to make a reasonable livelihood here, despite the fact that the cost of living here must be the highest in Britain due to the island's remoteness. One visiting departmental official, deploring the ever-rising inflation, declared that we islanders were lucky, it didn't affect us, we could "live off the hill" – a misconception shared by all who haven't tried it. But it is true we can, if necessary, tolerate a low standard of living. Our food is there to keep us alive, our clothes to keep us warm and dry. We don't need the elaborate cults of fancy food fads or the latest way-out fashions that others seem to consider so important for the titillation of their jaded senses. We may sometimes be frustrated, irritated, infuriated, driven to despair by our isle but we are never bored.

Modern industrial society, if it is to be efficient economically, requires its people to conform to a uniform standard. Its bureaucracy has no use for the small group whose needs are different, who cannot be tidily lumped in with the others. An insidious pressure is brought to bear on the local sub-cultures through the mass media, advertising and education to homogenize. The result – a drab uniformity spreads slowly over the world. Places like this where life appears "different" become important because they provide variety, they become designated as areas of interest to cater for the recreation of the masses, and it is advocated that the locals be carefully preserved to provide colour. Even if Mr Man-in-the-Street doesn't actually travel to one of these "different" places at least his life can be brightened by dreams of "getting away from it all" and his imagination stimulated by dramatic stories of the Edge of the World.

It could be argued that it is of military importance that the island be inhabited, occupying as it does quite a strategic position off the west coast of Shetland. It is feasible that if the island was uninhabited a foreign power could establish a base here for sabotage of the oil industry without any fear of discovery. Obviously it would be cheaper for this country to maintain the present population rather than build and man a precautionary military base. It might also be argued that the habitation of small outlying islands such as Foula, should play an important part in extending the hoped for EEC Fishing Limits to the maximum distance.

It *is* important to maintain the communities in the remoter parts of the country. If you allow Foula to be depopulated, are you to allow the same thing to happen to Shetland, or to the whole of the Highlands and Islands, eventually to the whole of rural Britain? Are we to end up with the country's entire population living only in the major cities? If not where are we to draw the line. Is not Foula as important to Shetland as Shetland is to the rest of Britain?

The above arguments might convince those already inclined in our favour. They won't convince the others. I know there must be an answer far more important than these, one that would be irrefutable, one which if presented to the world would bring help to our problems. I thought that if I wrote a book I would find it. But I didn't. I only found love and that is not enough.

But sometimes in the heart hole of winter as I platch knee deep through the mud on my way to the banks to hoove another dead ewe into the sea, it comes to me that maybe there is no reason, that it is of no importance, the world will not miss us. And I look out over the windswept sodden landscape to another time when we and our descendants will have passed away, when the isle perhaps will lie empty or populated by a people far different than our own. But then I look to the hills, black defiant against the winter sky, or out to sea where the big grey breakers roll by from the north and I know it does not matter. Long, long after we are gone from this world, the isle will still be our island. The wind will still roar through the hills, the seas still pound against its cliffs. The isle does not need us, it can stand alone. This is our sorrow and our comfort.

St. Cuthbert's

On this tiny island where the great saint came to struggle with his demons and converse with God, Peter Mortimer, a non-believer spending 100 days on the adjacent Holy Island, finds that God remains silent to him but nonetheless feels that this 'testing time' of solitude and Biblical reading has an indefinable value.

I Realized I Was No Saint

Peter Mortimer

For what reason was I planning my Three Tides for Cuthbert?

I had no real answer to this. Except it was all to do with me, my time on this island (Lindisfarne), the whole religion thing. Would that do?

Packing my bag for the first tide, I felt strangely nervous. I had two books, a flask of cocoa, crisps, binoculars, chocolate, a plastic sheet from George Ward, two black bin liners. Oh, and Charlie the black Labrador.

St Cuthbert had gone to the island for solitude, to find God, to fight demons. He finally retreated to the even more remote Farne Islands to the south-west. Poet Andrew Waterhouse had remarked (quite wisely) that anyone who spent that much time in isolation would find it hard to differentiate between the voice of God and hallucination.

My first tide was in daylight and the day itself had dawned bright and sunny. I wasn't fooled and pulled on two pairs of socks.

Once across that channel there was no return. Soon the water would be knee-deep, then waist-deep and finally neck-deep. Cuthbert was reputed to have stood hours long in this deep channel, casting out demons, which would need to be pretty hardy to survive anyway.

The island was bleak terrain, tortured volcanic rock on the top of which was tufted spongy grass whose uneven surface and hidden potholes made walking difficult. The stone remains of Cuthbert's cell were slightly sunken, offering some slight protection from the wind which was, it appeared, on a 24-hour-a-day, 7-day-a-week contract.

How big was the island? You could probably throw a cricket ball from one end to the other. Were you so inclined.

The sky seemed massive. The view back to Holy Island took in the Priory ruins, St Mary's church and the row of desirable properties named Fiddler's Green. Through the binoculars I could trace the progress of the Dinky-sized cars on the distant causeway. This would continue till 11.30 a.m. To the west, across the water, lay the mass of the Northumberland mainland.

Despite being several hundred yards from Holy Island proper, St Cuthbert's offered little privacy. Strollers up high on the Heugh could look over and down, and on various occasions during my stay I found myself eyeballing them, binoculars to binoculars. The Fiddler's Green properties could also see almost everything you did.

The island was almost litter-free; one light bulb, one plastic water bottle. A solitary fisherman's box had been washed up on the rocks and I watched as the tide slowly edged up to reclaim it.

The wind was south-west, which meant the most sheltered spot was crouched down right opposite the imposing cross, whose presence seemed to be demanding some reverence.

To appease it, I opened the Book of Psalms.

It had probably been 40 years since I'd read any Psalms. I suspect I was not alone. I read 80 of them. At times the blank verse was akin to declamatory poetry or even rap, and I could imagine them declaimed before a frenzied audience.

The Psalms were capable of creating extreme reactions – as in Waco, Texas – but to be fair so too were Leeds United. God was pretty vengeful and warlike – in Psalm 4 he will 'break the teeth of the wicked' and in Psalm 11 'on the wicked he will rain fiery coals and burning sulphur'. In this edition, the word LORD was always in uppercase. There was a great amount of uncritical adulation of said LORD, such as in Psalm 42: 'as the deer pants for you, so my soul pants for you, O LORD'.

Too much of this kind of thing, I thought, and the LORD might just get a wee bit bored. Good and evil in the Psalms was as cut and dried as in a standard western. At times, the imagery was beautiful, as in Psalm 65: 'The grasslands of the desert overflows/The hills are clothed with gladness/The meadows are covered with flocks/And the valleys are mantled with corn/They shout for joy and sing'. Without a single mention of the LORD.

I was crouched down into the shelter. I read a bit, snoozed a bit, drank some cocoa. I nibbled. Whenever Charlie spotted someone on Holy Island, he barked. On one occasion, through the binoculars, I tracked a nun making her way to the prayer holes where I'd cast my bread upon the water. She sat for a few minutes, then went back. Whether this was due to Charlie's barking or the deteriorating weather was unclear.

The wind was keener. The gloom intensified. I thought no more about reading. I drank the last of the cocoa, savouring its precious heat. My limbs began to stiffen. Occasionally I would stand and walk about but I was then at the mercy of the ever-growing wind which, on this exposed island, met no resistance. The walks were brief.

The extreme weather forced me at 5 p.m. to make two attempts to wade across the shrinking channel. Twice I was forced back as the water lapped over the wellie tops. By this time my body was shaking with the cold, my clothes were wet and St Cuthbert's Island had lost a small amount of its appeal. My breath was frosted and my limbs moved stiffly.

At 5.30 p.m. Mike Burden appeared on the shore and whistled for Charlie. The dog was fast off the blocks and weaved his way through the water like a dolphin. And if Charlie could go, I could go, wet socks or not. I'd had enough. And I'd lost my mate. I set off.

Before I reached the channel's middle, water was flooding into the wellies. I didn't give a damn. I needed warmth, shelter. I made my way home, ran a hot bath and lit the fire.

My original plan had been to spend three consecutive tides on the island. This would have been total folly and would have entailed returning to St Cuthbert's in five hours' time for another eight-hour exposure – this time through the night. My body would not have taken it. Superman apart, no one's would.

Part of me was miserable, dejected, another part sensed this testing time on the island had been worthwhile, even necessary to my Holy Island stay. But I had to accept the three tides would need to be staggered. Not for the first time in my life, I realised I was no saint.

Islands

John MacLeod writes defiantly on behalf, not only of the Gaels, but also of all small island communities who, despite everything, have endured and thrived 'on the edge'.

But Still We Sing

John MacLeod

We survive, despite the myths you all so stubbornly hold. You think we do not value nor enjoy our land, and that all we say is "You can't live on scenery", and that you are giving us a good example when you come a-holidaying amongst the blooming heather and silver lochs and crisp air and glowing evenings. But we love the earth and rocks about us; no-one appreciates the scenery more than those who live here. You like to think we are laid-back and slothful, but if we were, these hills and Hebrides would have been empty long since. You say that we are especially prone to mental illness; that we have a very high rate of drunkenness and alcoholism; that we go in either for manic boozing or manic religion. These are tabloid fantasies. Our religion, which still impacts our communities, seems preferable to your own non-religion that does not. So our elders burned fiddles? But your bishops burned people. And there is no statistical proof whatever that we are any more prone to depression or addiction than yourselves.

We see things differently; that is why our community life survives, while yours in the South is largely dead. We have time for people, for children; for strangers: time to smile or wave or stop for a crack in the road. We remember the widows. We revere our old. We entertain strangers. We care about our islands and villages and what becomes of them; we know little of other villages, far less of other Hebrides, but we know our own intimately and we love it passionately. We think of time, and we are most conscious of it – not in the hypertensive, rushing, frenzied sense of shortage that bedevils your world, but in its great and majestic and humbling sweep, time gone and time now and time to come. So we carry tradition and wisdom from our past, and preserve the memory of our people and family-lines, and look to preserve it and the land for our children and their children, and we watch the tide and the passing of the seasons, and think how little in ourselves we are.

You come to our townships and complain about our "junk" – rusting old cars and tractors, heaps of scrap, mouldering sheds crammed with this and that. But to us these things are beautiful in another way: faithful old motors that served us well, that deserve to rust in peace and can remain a communal resource for spare parts and useful bits of metal. You mock our Sabbath, where we still honour it: but you would enjoy it, if you were not always wanting to dash and to do, and entered into that rest and felt it give rhythm to your days and renewing to your bones.

We have survived. We know the weather, and the moor, and the sea, and the rocks; we know how things are done, and who should be doing them, and our communities hum about you with unseen energy and efficiency: watching, talking, deciding, acting. We have survived: though many must leave, many will return, and in the meantime they support the old ones at home, and link our township with its shadow in the great city, that urban tangle of Gaels, in churches and in the ballrooms.

We are in a new world order now. It is one that combines the comforts and technology of the modern with the human values of our past. Though we may at times combine it badly, and suffer the stresses and tensions of change, we are getting there. To function in this world, we need – and use – English, because language is a means to communicate, and everyone now speaks English, and gey few today have Gaelic, and the most of them better in English anyway. Do not expect us to stick with an outmoded tongue – man, you would have us back in the black houses if you could, the more quaint for you on your summer holiday. And do not make a moral issue of the thing, as if we were murdering a body; linguistic despotism is never pretty.

We have survived, though persecuted and belittled; we have survived in this land, and survived the attentions and tyrannies of yourselves.

BIOGRAPHIES

Anna Adams was born in 1936. She has published many collections of poetry. *Island Chapters* (1991) which records her years living on the tiny island of Scarp, in the Outer Hebrides.

J.M. Barrie (1860-1937) was born in Kirriemuir, the son of a handloom weaver. His most famous play, Peter Pan was first performed in 1904. Barrie lived for a time on the Isle of Harris, in the Outer Hebrides, as well as on Eilean Shona.

John Betjeman (1906-84) was born in Highgate. He was appointed Poet Laureate in 1972. He edited a number of Shell Guides to the British Isles. He had a great love for British landscape and architecture.

Ronald Blythe was born in 1922 and lives on the border between Suffolk and Essex. He is one of England's most eminent men of letters. The best known of his numerous books is entitled *Akenfield: Portrait of an English Village* (1969).

Heinrich Böll (1917-85) was one of Germany's most eminent 20th century novelists. He received the Nobel Prize for literature in 1972. He had a great love for Ireland in general and for Achill Island in particular.

Margaret Brockley was born in Jersey in 1935. She was just six years of age when her island was invaded by German forces. The nightmare experiences of life under Nazi rule have remained vividly with her all her life.

Iain Crichton Smith (1928-98) was born in Glasgow but moved to the Isle of Lewis when he was two. He lived with his crofter grandmother in the village of Babel. His Lewis childhood, dominated by the rigid doctrines of the Free church, haunts his poems.

David Clensy is an award winning Welsh journalist who spent time in the Cistercian monastery on Caldey Island which lies off the Pembrokeshire coast.

Kevin Crossley-Holland was born in Buckinghamshire in 1941 but now lives in North Norfolk. He is a poet and a successful children's author. His *Pieces of Land* (1972) is a record of journeys to eight British islands.

Catherine Czerkawska was born of Polish, Irish and English parentage and she moved to Scotland when she was twelve. She is a writer of novels, plays and short stories.

Tom Davies was born in Pontypridd in 1941. A former journalist, he has written novels and books of travel and Celtic pilgrimage.

Jane Dawson was born in Lincolnshire in 1942. She and her husband, Rod moved to the Hebridean island of Islay in 1974. Their small estate on the windswept Rhinns became a haven for wildlife.

Roger Deakin (1943-2006) lived in a Suffolk Elizabethan house, with a moat, which he rebuilt himself. He was an author and environmentalist. His best-known book is *Waterlog: A Swimmer's Journey Through Britain* (1999).

Catherine Duncan is an authority on the work of the great American photographer, Paul Strand. She wrote *Paul Strand: The World On My Doorstep* (1994).

John Fowles (1926-2005) was an eminent novelist who had a great love for islands. He once said that writing is the most difficult thing in the world and takes great courage.

Sheila Gear has lived for most of her life in Foula, Britain's remotest inhabited island,where she runs the island's post office.

Geoffrey Grigson (1905-85) was a poet, critic, editor and travel writer. A great deal of his work celebrates his native Cornwall.

Jim Hewitson is an author, journalist and broadcaster who lives on the Orkney island of Papa Westray. One of his many books is entitled, *Papa Westray: Island At The Rainbow's End* (1996).

James Hunter was born and brought up in Duror, Argyll and now lives in Skye. He is a journalist, broadcaster and award-winning writer who wrote the classic *The Making Of The Crofting Community* (1976).

Roger Hutchinson is an award winning journalist and author who now lives on the Isle of Raasay. His first book was entitled *The Soap Man: Lewis, Harris And Lord Leverhulme* (2005).

Kathleen Jamie was born in 1962 in Renfrewshire. She is one of Scotland's leading contemporary poets and a number of her poems are inspired by Hebridean islands. She currently teaches creative writing at St. Andrews University.

Bill Lawson has lived on the Isle of Harris, in the Outer Hebrides, for many years. He has written numerous books about inhabited and uni-habited Hebridean islands. He and his wife, Chris, run an exhibition centre in Northton.

Margaret Leigh worked on crofts in the 1930s in the Highlands and Islands. She was the author of a number of classic rural books such as *Highland Homespun* (1936) and *Spade Among The Rushes* (1949).

John Lister-Kaye is a naturalist and author who once worked with Gavin Maxwell. He runs a Field Centre for environmental education at Aigas in the Scottish Highlands.

Hugh MacDiarmid (1892-1978) was born in Langholm in the Scottish borders. His great poem written in synthetic Scots, *A Drunk Man Looks At The Thistle* appeared in 1926. He and his wife and children lived most of the 1930s on the Shetland island of Whalsay.

Neil MacGillvray was a boatman and gardener on the tiny island of Inchkenneth once owned by the Mitford family. He now lives on the neighbouring island of Mull.

George MacKay Brown (1921-96) was born and brought up in Orkney and rarely left the islands. He wrote many poems, stories and novels. His book *Orkney Tapestry* (1969) inspired Peter Maxwell Davies to find a home in Orkney.

Charles MacLean is the son of the war hero and author, Sir Fitzroy MacLean. He grew up in Argyll and writes fiction and non-fiction. His best known non-fiction work is *St. Kilda: Island On The Edge Of The World*, reissued in 1996.

Sorley MacLean (1911-60) was born on the island of Raasay. He was headmaster of Plocton High School for many years. He is regarded as one of the finest Gaelic poets of the 20th century.

John MacLeod is an author and controversial columnist who now lives in Lewis in the Outer Hebrides. His latest book entitled, *Banner In The West: A Spiritual History Of Lewis And Harris* is due to be published in 2008.

Louis MacNeice (1907-63) was born in Belfast, the son of a rector who became a bishop. He was a writer-producer for the BBC for a number of years. Along with W.H. Auden, he was one of the leading British poets of the 1930s and 1940s.

Gavin Maxwell (1914-69) was born in Monreith in the Scottish Borders but had a lifelong passion for the Highlands and Islands. His best known book, *Ring Of Bright Water* (1960) was made into a popular film.

Rosemary Millington is an Australian writer whose first book entitled, *A Nation Of Trees* (1964) was described as one of the finest books written on Australia.

Peter Mortimer is a playwright, poet and editor who also writes travel-type books. His novella *Uninvited* is due from Red Squirrel Press in 2009. *Off the Wall – The Journey of a Play* was published 2008, Five Leaves Publications.

Edwin Muir (1887-1959) was born on the main island of Orkney but moved to the tiny island of Wyre when he was an infant. He is one of the finest Scottish poets to have written in English. *An Autobiography* (1954) beautifully evokes his island childhood.

Richard Murphy was born in County Mayo in 1972. He bought High Island which lies off the west coast of Ireland and lived there alone for a number of years. Many of his poems deal with life on the island.

Adam Nicholson is a prolific author and his family still own the Shiants, a small group of islands in the Outer Hebrides, which he movingly describes in his book, *Sea Room* (2002).

Winifred Nicholson (1893-1981) was a distinguished painter who made frequent trips to the Hebridean islands of Eigg and Canna in the 1940s and 50s, often accompanied by her friend, Kathleen Raine.

Liam O'Flaherty (1896-1984) was born on the Aran Islands. A novelist and great short story writer. In many of his stories, he writes with extraordinary insight about the life and death of animals.

George Orwell (1903-50) was born in Bengal but brought to England at an early age. Just after the Second World War, he moved to the island of Jura, one of the largest and emptiest Hebridean islands, where he wrote most of *Nineteen Eighty-Four* (1949).

Michael Powell (1905-90) was one of Britain's most eminent film directors. His *Edge Of The World* (1936), based on the evacuation of the islanders of St.Kilda, was filmed on the Shetland island of Foula.

Kathleen Raine (1908-2003) was the daughter of a Scottish mother and a Northumbrian father. Much of her poetry is inspired by the Hebridean

Islands where she experienced a sense of the sacred.

Peig Sayers (1873-1958) spent the greater part of her life on Great Blasket. She was one of a number of great Gaelic storytellers who kept the island's traditions alive.

Alistair Scott is a Scottish born travel writer who has written numerous books about his travels throughout the world. His latest book, *Sea and Emerald* (2008) describes his solo voyage around Ireland.

Mike Seabrook is an author best-known for his biography of the leading contemporary composer, Sir Peter Maxwell Davies, *Max: The Life And Music Of Peter Maxwell Davies* (1994).

Margaret Fay Shaw (1902-2003) grew up in Pennsylvania. She lived for six years on South Uist and collected the island's traditional Gaelic songs and folk lore. She lived on the Hebridean island of Canna for many years until her death.

Stella Shepherd arrived on the tiny Shetland island of Papa Stour in the 1960s to take up the joint roles of teacher and missionary.

Christopher Somerville is a writer and broadcaster who has written a great deal about life in remote rural and island communities.

J.M. Synge (1871-1909) was born near Dublin. At the suggestion of W. B. Yeats, he went to live on the Aran Islands between 1898 and 1902 and life on those islands came to have a profound influence on his dramas.

R. S. Thomas (1913-2000) was born in Cardiff. He was ordained as a priest in the Church of Wales in 1936. This distinguished poet once stayed for a few days on the Hebridean island of Soay where Gavin Maxwell once lived.

Deborah Tall is an American poet who lived for a year on Inishbofin in the 1980s.

Mike Tomkies is a naturalist, writer and film maker. A former Hollywood journalist, he has written many books about his life in remote and wild places in the Scottish Highlands, Canada and Spain.

Virginia Woolf (1882-1941) was born at Hyde Park Gate. After her father's death, she and her sister and brothers moved to Bloomsbury where they formed the nucleus of the Bloomsbury Group. Her best known novel, *To The Lighthouse* (1927) was ostensibly based on the Isle of Skye.

David Yeadon is a distinguished American travel writer who has written more than twenty books about traveling around the world, including the *National Geographic Guide to the World's Secret Places* (2004).

W.B. Yeats (1865-1939) was born in Dublin. During his time at the School of Art, he developed an interest in mystic religion and the supernatural. He is considered one of the greatest poets of the 20th century.

James Knox Whittet (*Editor*) was born and brought up in the Hebridean island of Islay where his father was the head gardener at a small castle. His paternal grandmother was from a crofting family on the Isle of Skye. He was educated at Keills Primary, Newbattle Abbey College and Cambridge University. His *Seven Poems For Engraved Fishermen*, with engravings by John Richter, was shortlisted for an award by the National Library of Scotland. In 2004, 2005 and in 2008, he won the George Crabbe Memorial Award. In 2005 he edited the anthology entitled *100 Island Poems Of Great Britain and Ireland* for IRON Press which was nominated as one of the Books of the Year by *The Scotsman*.

Index of Authors

ACKNOWLEDGEMENTS

Anna Adams, *Island Chapters* (Arc 1991) extract reprinted by permission of author.

J. M. Barrie, *Letters Of J.M. Barrie,* Peter Davies, London, 1942.

John Betjeman, *John Betjeman: Coming Home* by Candida Lycett Green, Methuen, London, 1997.

Ronald Blythe, *Going To Meet George* (Long Barn 1999) extract reprinted by permission of author.

Heinrich Böll, *Irish Journal,* Random House, London, 2000.

Margaret Brockley, *From Auschwitz To Alderney* by Tom Freeman-Keel, Seer Publishing, Shropshire, 1995.

George MacKay Brown, *For The Islands I Sing,* John Murray, London, 1997.

David Clensy, *Hold The Front Page,* Northcliffe, London, 2000.

Kevin Crossley-Holland, *Pieces Of Land* (Victor Gollancz 1972) extract reprinted by permission of author.

Catherine Czerkawska, *God's Islanders* (Birlinn 2006) extract reprinted by permission of author.

Tom Davies, *Wild Skies And Celtic Paths* (Triangle Books 1998) extracts reprinted by permission of SPCK Publishing & Sheldon Press.

Jane Dawson, *Long Tales* (Lag Mhor Oifis 2004) extract reprinted by permission of author.

Roger Deakin, *Waterlog* (Chatto & Windus1999) extract reprinted by permission of the Random House Group Ltd.

John Fowles, *Islands,* Jonathan Cape, London, 1978.

Sheila Gear, *Foula: Island West Of The Sun* (Robert Hale 1983) extract reprinted by permission of author.

Geoffrey Grigson, *Country Writings,* Century Publishing, London, 1984

Jim Hewitson, *Clinging To The Edge* (Mainstream 1996) extract reprinted by permission of author.

James Hunter, *Scottish Highlanders: A People And Their Place* (Mainstream 1992) extract reprinted by permission of author.

Roger Hutchinson, *Calum's Road* (Birlinn 2006) extract reprinted by permission of Birlinn Ltd. www.birlinn.co.uk

Kathleen Jamie, *Island At The Edge Of The World* (The Saturday Guardian, 26th August, 2006) extract reprinted by permission of author.

Bill Lawson, *Harris In History And Legend* (Birlinn 2002) extract reprinted by permission of author.

Margaret Leigh, *Driftwood And Tangle*, Macmillan, London, 1941.

John Lister-Kaye, *The White Island* (Pan Books 1976) extract reprinted by permission of author.

Hugh MacDiarmid, *Lucky Poet* (Jonathan Cape 1972) extract reprinted by permission of the Random House Group Ltd.

Neil MacGillvray, *When I Was Young: The Islands*, by Timothy Neat, (Birlinn 2000) extract reprinted by permission of Birlinn Ltd.

Charles MacLean, *St.Kilda: Island On The Edge Of The World* (Canongate 1996) extract reprinted by permission of Canongate.

Sorley MacLean, *From Wood To Ridge* (Vintage 1991) extract reprinted by permission of Carcanet.

John MacLeod, *No Great Mischief If You Fall* (Mainstream 1993) extract reprinted by permission of Mainstream.

Louis MacNeice, *I Crossed The Minch*, Longmans, Green & Co. London, 1938.

Gavin Maxwell, *Harpoon At A Venture*, Rupert Hart-Davis,London 1952.

Rosemary Millington, *The Islanders*, The Anchor Press, Essex, 1967.

Peter Mortimer, *100 Days On Holy Island* (Mainstream 2002) extract reprinted by permission of author.

Edwin Muir, *An Autobiography* (The Hogarth Press 2008) extract reprinted by permission of Canongate.

Richard Murphy, *A Kick: A Life Among Writers* (Granta Books 2002) extract reprinted by permission of Granta Books.

Adam Nicholson, *Atlantic Britain* (HarperCollins 2004) extract reprinted by permission of HarperCollins.

Winifred Nicholson, *Unknown Colour: Paintings, Letters, Writings by Winifred Nicholson*, Ed. Andrew Nicholson, Faber, London, 1987.

Liam O'Flaherty, *Shame The Devil*, Wolfhound Press, Dublin, 1934.

George Orwell, *The Collected Essays, Journalism And Letters* (Martin Secker

& Warburg 2007) extract reprinted by permission of Godine.

Michael Powell, *The Isle Of Foula* by Prof. IBS Holburn, Birlinn, Edinburgh, 2001.

Kathleen Raine, *The Land Unknown,* Hamilton, London, 1975.

Peig Sayers, *An Old Woman's Reflections* (Oxford University Press 1962) extract reprinted by permission of the Oxford University Press.

Alistair Scott, *Native Stranger* (Little, Brown & Company 1995) extract reprinted by permission of Little, Brown Book Group.

Mike Seabrook, *Max: The Life And Music Of Peter Maxwell Davies,* Victor Gollancz, London, 1994.

Margaret Fay Shaw, *From The Alleghenies To The Hebrides* (Birlinn 2004) extract reprinted by permission of Birlinn Ltd.

Stella Shepherd, *Like A Mantle The Sea* (The Shetland Times, Lerwick 1985) extract reprinted by permission of The Shetland Times.

Iain Crichton Smith, (Iona) Extract from *Scotland On Sunday Magazine,* Edinburgh, 1991, (Lewis) *Towards The Human,* MacDonald, Edinburgh, 1986.

Christopher Somerville, *The Road To Roaring Water* (HarperCollins 1993) extract reprinted by permission of HarperCollins.

J. M. Synge, *The Aran Islands,* Oxford University Press, Oxford, 1992.

Deborah Tall, *The Island Of The White Cow,* André Deutsch, London, 1986.

R.S. Thomas, Extract from *Autobiographies,* Orion Books, London, 1998

Mike Tomkies, *Between Earth And Paradise* (Whittles, Caithness 2005) extract reprinted by permission of Whittles.

Virginia Woolf, *Congenial Spirits: Selected Letters Of Virginia Woolf,* Ed. Joanne Trautmann Banks, The Hogarth Press, London, 1989.

David Yeadon, *Seasons On Harris,* HarperCollins, New York, 2006.

W. B. Yeats, *Essays And Introductions,* Macmillan, London, 1961.